seriously
simple
parties

seriously simple parties

RECIPES, MENUS & ADVICE
FOR EFFORTLESS ENTERTAINING

diane rossen worthington

PHOTOGRAPHS BY YVONNE DUIVENVOORDEN

CHRONICLE BOOKS
SAN FRANCISCO

Text copyright © 2012
by Diane Rossen Worthington.
Photographs copyright © 2012
by Yvonne Duivenvoorden.

Library of Congress
Cataloging-in-Publication Data available.

ISBN 978-0-8118-7257-7

Manufactured in China

Designed by Laura Palese
Prop styling by Catherine Doherty
Food styling by Lucie Richard
Production management by Sarah Lichter

10 9 8 7 6 5 4 3 2 1

Chronicle Books LLC
680 Second Street
San Francisco, California 94107
www.chroniclebooks.com

acknowledgments

Ethan Ellenberg, my agent, who is always available with a creative thought

Bill LeBlond, my supportive editor, who is always there to listen to my ideas

Amy Treadwell, for her helpful editorial input and creative thinking, which have helped me solve organizational challenges

Joanna Ramos, for her skilled assistance in the kitchen and her sense of humor

Jill Kanofsky, for all of her recipe assistance, testing, and help at a moment's notice

Anthony Dias Blue, whose expert knowledge is reflected in the wine pairing advice

Denny Luria, for her lifelong friendship and thoughtful insights and for always being there

Laurie Burrows Grad, Kathy Blue, Janice Wald Henderson, Ciji Ware, my cooking colleagues and dear friends, for all of their input

Mary Beth Rose; Lucy Suzar; Connie Bryson; Judy, Kenny, Sam, and Ali Miller; Lisa and Steve Hillman; Cathi and George Rimalower; and Ruth and Don Salk for being great tasters and critics

And last but not least, my husband, Michael, and my daughter, Laura, who always make me laugh.

for laura
& michael,
who give
me reason
to celebrate

contents

introduction

I wrote *Seriously Simple* in 2002 to help the busy home cook spend as little time as possible in the kitchen while still creating tasty dishes. My recipes had as much to do with lifestyle as they did with flavor. They were designed to minimize prep time and streamline cooking techniques, while retaining the pleasing, complex flavors of more labor-intensive dishes.

The recipes I created seemed to resonate with my readers, and *Seriously Simple Holidays* followed soon after. In response to that book, repeated e-mails to my Seriously Simple Web site raised questions about entertaining. My readers wanted to know how to throw a party without becoming overwhelmed by all the planning, shopping, prep work, cooking, and serving. Is it possible to do it all without calling in the troops? I love to entertain and have many tips to share, having learned from my own mistakes over the years. So I decided to write *Seriously Simple Parties,* a collection of recipes that are meant to reduce that all-too-common feeling of party anxiety.

This book will show you how to pull together a festive meal for a small or large group that is tasty and beautifully presented, but doesn't require endless hours of preparation. I've developed recipes based on fresh ingredients, shortcut cooking techniques, and a well-stocked pantry to enable you to throw a party with a minimum of effort.

The most important requirement for a successful party is organization.

Years of entertaining have shown me that careful organization ahead of time makes for the best event. Preplanning allows me to spend time talking and relaxing with my guests, instead of working in the kitchen. Whether I am preparing a meal for 4 or 12, planning ahead and making to-do lists is my secret to an enjoyable get-together.

1. Decide what kind of gathering you want to have.

The section on Party Entertaining Styles (page 23) will help you select from a range of options, whether it's a sit-down brunch for 6, an outdoor buffet dinner for 12, or a family-style luncheon for 10, where all the dishes appear on the table at the same time.

2. Choose your menu.

Seriously Simple Parties provides a variety of menus (pages 31 to 45) for a range of different kinds of entertaining. The menus are meant as suggestions: feel free to make changes to suit your own taste. Note that the menus and recipes are arranged by season, so your dishes will include the freshest ingredients currently available.

3. Select your beverages.

See Stocking the Bar (page 26) to organize the drinks for your party. I describe how to figure out the amounts of wine and liquor you'll need, depending on the size of your gathering. Check out the Beverages chapter (page 47), and choose from a number of creative cocktails to help get the party going.

LISTS AND SCHEDULES

Menu and Cooking Schedule
List all the dishes you will serve at your party, and note when each one will be made. You may decide to do some steps well in advance, and others a day or two before the party. Also note any last-minute touches that will need to be added.

Shopping and Chores Schedule
Arrange a schedule for buying flowers, desserts, or other last-minute purchases. Coordinate any final tasks for party prep, including lighting the candles, refrigerating wines and drinks, and getting ice ready. Note any family member or friend who can do the task.

Drinks and Other Nonperishables Shopping List
Note all the nonperishables you need, from the wine to the centerpieces. These can be bought a week or so ahead.

Perishables Shopping List
The list should include all the fresh food you will need, such as salad ingredients and other vegetables, cheeses, and meats. Purchase fruit that needs to ripen at least a couple of days ahead of your event. Decide what flowers you will need and purchase them a few days ahead of your event.

Tabletop Items
The dishes, tablecloths, napkins, silverware, serving pieces, and candles you plan to use should be included in this list. You might want to think about where people will sit, and even make place cards for a more formal gathering.

4. Check and replenish your pantry.

Having your staples on hand is key to hassle-free party prep. The Party Pantry (page 13) will help you stock your cupboard with ingredients that are essential for my recipes. For example, you will appreciate having a good selection of red and white vinegars and assorted oils when making salad dressings, sautés, and sauces. Keeping good-quality chicken or vegetable stocks and canned tomatoes within reach will make soup and stew prep that much easier. A selection of chocolates and nuts will give you the freedom to throw together cookies or cakes without having to make another trip to the store.

5. Make those lists!

They may seem like extra work, but careful planning will save you time and make entertaining seriously simple. I think of these lists as my road map to a successful party, a strategy that takes the stress out of pulling everything together.

6. Prep kitchen a week or two before the party.

Space out your cooking tasks. My recipes always offer tips for advance preparation, which will make your work more manageable. A sauce can be made a week in advance and frozen until you're ready to use it. The first couple of steps of many recipes can be completed days ahead. As the day of your party draws near, remember the Seriously Simple philosophy: keep it fresh and keep it simple. That means if you don't have time to prepare all the dishes you want to serve, don't panic. Feel free to pick up a fresh store-bought item instead.

There are so many reasons to celebrate.
I'm big on informal gatherings like a family-style dinner or a casual midday brunch. I also look forward to annual parties like my Academy Awards dinner or a Super Bowl Sunday lunch. And I love to throw parties celebrating family moments like a graduation or anniversary dinner. I believe that if there's an occasion, that's a good reason for a celebration. And if there's no occasion, arrange a get-together and create one.

Just know that when you choose to entertain, you are not alone. You can rely on my book as your friend in the kitchen and at the party.

have fun,
diane

party
basics

the party pantry

The Seriously Simple Party Pantry is all about having straightforward, uncomplicated ingredients on hand that can make a bold impact, even when you are putting together only a few simple dishes for an impromptu get-together. Many of these ingredients will keep for a long time in your pantry, refrigerator, or freezer.

agave syrup

A healthier alternative to sugar, agave is a great sweetener to use in homemade drinks and desserts. You can use it in place of simple syrup.

apricot jam

Use the jam for brushing on finished pastry.

baking powder

Look for double-acting aluminum-free brands. Store in a cool dry place for up to 6 months. After that, baking powder loses its effectiveness.

baking soda

Store in a cool dry place for up to 6 months.

broths

In recent years premade chicken, vegetable, and beef broths have drastically improved. They are great time-savers and are perfect for homemade soups, stews, and sauces. Select broths in paper cartons so you can store the leftovers easily in the refrigerator for a few days. You can also freeze small quantities for a few months and use them for sauces or stir-fries. Look for low-sodium broths so you can control the amount of salt going into your dish.

butter

I use unsalted butter because it has no preservatives and has an excellent flavor. I always have a few pounds in my freezer for any last-minute cooking, since it keeps so well.

capers

These piquant buds are available either packed in brine or salt. Make sure to rinse them well. Try these as an added flavor enhancer in salads, dressing, and sauces, and as a simple garnish.

cheese

Cheese is a fantastic party food because it is so versatile. It can be a course all on its own, with just a few accompaniments, or it can be a component in salads, entrées, and even desserts.

BLUE CHEESE: Domestic Maytag blue and Point Reyes blue, and imported Gorgonzola, Stilton, and Roquefort are all recommended.

BURRATA: The creamy cousin to mozzarella. Burrata means "buttered." This cheese has a mixture of cream and mozzarella curds in the center of each ball, and an outside layer of mozzarella that holds it together. It has a buttery, creamy flavor. Serve this cheese on its own as a first course or pair with olive tapenade or fresh or sun-dried tomatoes. It is also good wrapped with prosciutto or as a simple dessert drizzled with honey. Burrata is best eaten as fresh as possible.

CHEDDAR: The longer this cow's milk cheese is aged, the sharper and more complex the flavor will be. Look for an aged cheddar for both cooking and eating. Cheddar cheeses are usually white to pale yellow.

FETA: Traditionally made from sheep's or goat's milk, feta is now made with cow's milk, too. This white cheese is cured in brine, which accounts for its salty flavor. It is also slightly tangy and has a crumbly texture. Feta can range from soft to semidry. It is good in salads, pastas, and appetizers.

GOAT CHEESE: Domestic goat cheese is now readily available. Chèvre, or French goat cheese, is a bit stronger and more expensive. Fresh goat cheese is good served warm on salad or as an ingredient in cold salads and pasta sauces. Or try a log of fresh goat cheese coated in herbs as a dressed-up, simple hors d'oeuvre. As goat cheese ages, it becomes stronger and its character more pronounced.

MOZZARELLA: Fresh mozzarella is best used in salads and for cooking. It's a popular ingredient in pizza and pasta dishes because of its excellent melting qualities. Fresh mozzarella usually comes packed in water and is available in several sizes, including ciliegine, which are little balls. They're great in salads.

PARMESAN: Authentic Italian Parmesan, known as Parmigiano-Reggiano, is strictly licensed and has been produced in much the same way for almost seven hundred years. The cheese should be straw yellow in color and have a crumbly, moist texture. Look for the words *Parmigiano-Reggiano* stamped on the rind of the cheese. Store it in plastic in the refrigerator for up to 3 months. If it becomes dry, wrap it in moist cheesecloth and leave it in the refrigerator for a few hours. Then rewrap it in plastic. It's best to grate Parmesan as needed for optimum flavor.

PECORINO ROMANO: An Italian hard sheep's milk cheese that has a very sharp, pungent flavor. Aged pecorino ranges in color from white to pale yellow. Use it for grating for a stronger flavor than Parmesan.

PECORINO TUSCANO: A sheep's milk cheese that is considerably milder than Pecorino Romano, Pecorino Toscano is made throughout Tuscany. It is similar to Parmigiano, though it's a little creamier and has a distinctively bitter walnut undertone that balances its subtle sweetness, giving it added complexity. Aged Pecorino Toscano is also good cut into thin crumbly slices over foods. Try it with a sliced pear and a drizzle of orange honey or in any pasta dish that calls for Parmigiano-Reggiano.

PEPPER JACK: Like all Jack cheeses, it is a mild, semisoft cheese with a high moisture content. Pieces of chile peppers are added for a spicy flavor. (The cheese is sometimes named for its chile, such as jalapeño Jack or habanero Jack.) The longer the cheese is aged, the hotter and spicier it becomes.

WHITE TRUFFLE CHEESE: This is a semifirm sheep's and cow's milk cheese studded with bits of white truffle. The earthy white truffles mingle nicely with the sweet and tangy flavor of the cheese. Try it in grilled cheese sandwiches, potato gratin, and in mac and cheese.

chocolate

The cacao content of chocolate is the percentage of the chocolate that comes from the cocoa bean. The cocoa bean contains cocoa butter and chocolate liquor. When the percentage of cacao is high, there is more chocolate liquor and less cocoa butter. Sugar is added to bittersweet and semisweet chocolate, but not to unsweetened chocolate.

COCOA POWDER: Choose a good quality unsweetened cocoa powder, such as Scharffen Berger. I like it for its delicate flavor. It's great for baking and making hot chocolate.

SEMISWEET AND BITTERSWEET CHOCOLATE: Semisweet chocolate is usually around 60 percent cacao. Bittersweet is 65 to 75 percent cacao. Make sure to store all chocolate in a cool, dark place. For semisweet or bittersweet chocolate, I use imported Valrhona or Callebaut, or domestic Scharffen Berger or Ghirardelli.

UNSWEETENED CHOCOLATE: It is 100 percent cacao and consists entirely of chocolate liquor, with no added sugar. It is used in baking in combination with sugar or another sweetener. I like Scharffen Berger, Baker's, or Hershey's.

WHITE CHOCOLATE: There is no chocolate liquor in white chocolate. It does contain cocoa butter, which is why it is called white chocolate. The flavor is very mild, sweet, and creamy. I like Ghirardelli or Lindt. Use white chocolate for baking cakes, cookies, and muffins.

citrus

A little juice and zest from lemons, limes, or oranges can really brighten up the flavors in a dish, such as steamed vegetables or split pea soup. In the spring, consider using Meyer lemons and blood oranges for a unique flavor and, in the case of blood oranges, a surprising splash of red. A simple wedge or twist of citrus can also make the perfect party garnish for drinks, entrées, and desserts. Always keep citrus fruits on hand because even if you don't use all of them, they make a fabulous centerpiece in a bowl.

condiments

CHILI SAUCE: A tomato sauce that usually includes onion, green pepper, sugar, vinegar, and spices. It is a tasty base for cocktail sauce or for serving with meat. It also makes a good Thousand Island dressing with the addition of mayonnaise.

CHUTNEY: A spicy-sweet condiment that contains fruit (such as mango), vinegar, sugar, and spices. It can be chunky or smooth, mild or hot. A chutney makes a great accompaniment to main dishes, cheese platters, and appetizers.

FIG COMPOTE: Made with dried figs, sometimes other dried fruits, sugar, and wine, this compote is delicious with Brie and prosciutto as a sandwich or appetizer.

KETCHUP: It's always good to have your favorite brand on hand.

MAYONNAISE: A great helper in making aioli. Try light mayonnaise for a creamy texture without all of the calories.

MUSTARDS
Keep these three different mustards on hand.
  Dijon: Smooth, silky, and slightly tangy. Grey Poupon and Pommery are good brands.
  Honey mustard: Make sure this has a base of Dijon mustard, not the ballpark variety.
  Whole-grain mustard: Mustard with the hull of the mustard seed included.

TAPENADE: An olive spread that usually includes green or black olives, capers, anchovies, garlic, and olive oil. Add a tablespoon to mayonnaise or a vinaigrette for a Mediterranean touch.

cooking spray

A healthful alternative to oils and butter, cooking spray makes for easy cleanup and helps baked goods release from the pan.

ALL-PURPOSE: Great for keeping food from sticking to the grill or baking sheets.

BAKING: Made with flour, baking spray can replace the time-consuming and messy process of greasing and flouring baking pans and muffin tins.

OLIVE OIL: Helps you spray an even layer over bread, potatoes, vegetables, etc. so they can brown.

cream of coconut

Look for the Coco López brand. Cream of coconut is excellent in dessert sauces and cocktails.

dried fruits

Dried cranberries, cherries, apricots, figs, currants, and prunes are good pantry items to have in the winter months, when fresh fruit is not abundant. Use them to brighten up quick breads, muffins, sauces, rice, or stuffing. Dried cranberries, currants, and cherries can be used like raisins in baking and cooking. Plump them in boiling water or wine for about 20 minutes to bring out their full flavor.

dried mushrooms

Make sure mushrooms are tightly packaged. I like to use shiitake, porcini, or morels. To rehydrate the mushrooms, cover them with boiling water for 20 minutes before using.

figs

Fresh figs are available in the summer and fall months. Look for the deep purplish-black Black Mission, yellowish-green Kadota, brownish-purple Brown Turkey, or pale yellow Calimyrna. Any of these varieties are excellent for cooking or eating raw. Refrigerate until using.

flour

ALL-PURPOSE FLOUR, UNBLEACHED: This is used in most cooking and baking.

BREAD FLOUR: Higher in gluten than all-purpose, bread flour is used for making bread, pizza, and flatbread.

SEMOLINA FLOUR: A hard durum wheat ground into flour, which is yellow in color. High in gluten, semolina is excellent for making breads as well as pasta.

fresh herbs

Fresh herbs don't last long. During the growing season, cultivating your own small herb garden is the most cost-effective way to ensure that you always have fresh herbs. Fresh herbs are wonderful in everything from soups to vegetables and can really brighten up a dish. Fresh flat-leaf parsley, basil, and thyme are some of the most versatile.

frozen foods

Frozen vegetables and premade dough can be a time-saver for parties, and your guests will never know that these ingredients came straight from the freezer. They are convenient to keep on hand because frozen foods last a long time.

BERRIES: When berries are not in season, you can substitute frozen berries instead of buying expensive imports. Add whole frozen berries to Champagne or mixed drinks for an elegant touch.

EDAMAME: Select shelled frozen edamame, which is the Japanese word for green soybeans. Microwave and salt them for a great party snack or add them to sauces, such as pesto, and salads.

ICE CREAM AND SORBET: I always have French vanilla and mango sorbet in my freezer for last-minute desserts. A scoop of vanilla ice cream on a warm dessert always pleases.

PEAS: Look for petits pois that have been frozen at their peak of freshness. I use these peas in rice, pasta, soups, and as the foundation for a puréed pea sauce.

PIZZA CRUST: Many grocery stores now carry good-quality frozen pizza dough. You may also find fresh ready-made pizza dough at your local pizzeria.

PUFF PASTRY: I always keep a package in my freezer. Keep it simple by using frozen puff pastry for petite hors d'oeuvres or desserts that will wow your guests.

fruit nectars

I like to use guava, apricot, or peach nectar for drinks and marinades because of their concentrated flavor.

garlic

Prepeeled whole cloves of garlic is a great time-saver. For minced garlic, use a garlic press instead of chopping. Garlic is used in many cuisines, so is great to have on hand. Don't worry about the pungent flavor; garlic tends to mellow as it is cooked.

ginger

After you peel the ginger, you can shred or grate it or cut it into julienne strips. Do not substitute dried ginger for fresh.

grains and pasta

These are great to keep in your pantry because they will last a long time, and they can help make stellar hot or cold sides for parties any time of the year. Herbs, cheeses, and dried fruits and nuts are particularly good when tossed with the following grains and pasta.

ARBORIO RICE: This short-grain Italian rice is incredibly versatile. Arborio has a very high starch content, making it a favorite for preparing risotto. Other varieties like Vialone Nano or Carnaroli are also excellent. Risotto makes a great party food because it can be flavored in a variety of ways and made in large amounts.

BOMBA RICE: A Spanish short-grain rice that is recommended for making paella. It can absorb a great deal of liquid and still be perfectly cooked, with distinct grains.

ELBOW MACARONI: Best for making macaroni and cheese or Baked Greek Pasta (page 102).

ISRAELI COUSCOUS: These little balls made out of semolina and wheat flour are usually toasted and are slightly larger than other couscous grains. Choose regular or whole wheat.

ORZO: A variety of pasta shaped like large grains of rice. But unlike rice, it does not tend to stick together, making it a wonderful choice for cold pasta salads. Orzo is great when tossed with fresh herbs and can make the perfect side dish for meat or fish dishes.

QUINOA: A South American supergrain packed with nutrients. Quinoa is easy to prepare for crowds and has many uses. It is great served warm with meats and fish or cold in a salad, mixed with herbs and vegetables. Try cooking quinoa with vegetable or chicken broth instead of water to add extra flavor.

greek yogurt
Found in most well-stocked supermarkets, Greek yogurt is a thick and tangy plain yogurt. It makes a great marinade for chicken, lamb, or fish, and when combined with lemon and herbs, it makes a wonderful dipping sauce for crudités. Look for nonfat or 2 percent.

hoisin
A deep reddish-brown, thick, sweet and spicy sauce used in Chinese cooking. Hoisin sauce is made from soybeans, vinegar, garlic, sugar, chile peppers, and spices. It is available in jars in Asian markets and most supermarkets. It must be refrigerated once opened.

honey
There are many types of honey, and they vary in flavor and appearance. Some are thin while others are more like a firm paste. Honey can be white, golden, amber, brown, or even black. The most popular types are clover honey and orange blossom honey, both of which are suitable for cooking and baking. Look for lavender, sage, white truffle, or wildflower honey at specialty food stores and farmers' markets. These are wonderful drizzled on cheese and fruit. All honeys should be stored in tightly sealed containers, although eventually they will crystallize and harden with age. To soften the honey, place the jar in a bowl of hot water.

horseradish
Cream-style white horseradish is useful as a flavor enhancer for sauces, and it's also wonderful in Bloody Marys.

hot sauce
Just a little bit of heat can really add some spice to your party.

CHOLULA: Similar to Tabasco but with less vinegar, Cholula is good for adding heat to sauces, and it makes a great drizzle over egg dishes.

SRIRACHA: A Thai thick hot sauce that is great in dipping sauces and marinades.

TABASCO: A vinegary hot sauce that is perfect for adding heat to soups, chili, and many other dishes.

TABASCO CHIPOTLE: Chipotle peppers add a smoky flavor to this hot sauce, which can lend some depth to your sauces and barbecue foods.

maple syrup
Pure maple syrup gives a deep, complex sweetness to a variety of dishes, both savory and sweet. Try it in salad dressings, baked beans, nut tarts, plain yogurt, or warm cereal. I like using a good dark amber Grade B syrup for cooking, since the flavor is more intense than the lighter Grade A (which is best for pouring over pancakes). Look for pure maple syrup from producers in Canada, Vermont, or New Hampshire in specialty stores or online.

marzipan
A thick paste made of sugar and almonds. It is used in baking.

marinades

Marinades add flavor to whatever you're cooking. Most marinades are a combination of an acid—such as citrus juice, vinegar, wine, or even yogurt—and vegetable or olive oil. Spices, herbs, and mustards are often added for a distinctive flavor. Add a minimum of salt, since it can toughen the meat.

I like to use a ratio of 2 parts acid to 1 part oil. Use glass, porcelain, or enamel for marinating, since aluminum will give the food a metallic taste. Be sure all surfaces of the food are covered with the marinade. Some tips:

- Beef, veal, pork, and lamb can be marinated for up to 24 hours without any damage to their texture.
- Generally, poultry needs a shorter marinating time, up to 6 hours, and fish should never be marinated for more than 2 hours if the marinade is very acidic.
- Don't forget about marinating vegetables, which are particularly good grilled. Marinate vegetables for 30 minutes to 4 hours.
- If you are marinating food in the refrigerator, remove it 30 minutes before grilling so that it can come to room temperature.
- Use the marinade to baste food during cooking to give it extra moisture and flavor.
- Pastes and rubs (herb coatings) are marinades, too. Plan on spreading the paste on the meat, poultry, or seafood up to 4 hours ahead of cooking. A food covered with a paste that contains little acid can usually marinate for up to 8 hours.

nuts

Nuts are a great addition to any party. Season and toast them for hors d'oeuvres, add them to salads, use them in sauces or in desserts. Freeze by placing the nuts in a lock-top plastic bag after you open them.

ALMONDS: Select blanched whole or slivered almonds. And try whole Spanish Marcona almonds for something a little different. They are lightly fried and salted and have a uniquely rich, nutty flavor. Serve Marcona almonds as is with cocktails, or add them to your favorite vegetables or salads.

CANDIED PECANS, ALMONDS, OR WALNUTS: Great to have on hand for salads and as a sweet accompaniment for cheese and fruit desserts.

PECANS: Use pecan halves. Their buttery flavor tastes great in cookies and other desserts.

PISTACHIOS: Select raw shelled, unsalted pistachios, which are available in most supermarkets.

RAW UNSALTED MIXED NUTS: Pecans, walnuts, Brazil nuts, cashews, peanuts, and hazelnuts are great, warm, with drinks.

WALNUTS: Select walnut halves and freeze after opening.

olive oil

There are many types of olive oils, and they vary in flavor and color, depending on the olive variety, the climate and soil where the olives grow, and the amount of processing involved.

EXTRA-VIRGIN: These cold-pressed oils are usually fruity and green and possess a grassy, slightly bitter flavor. The oil is wonderful when used unheated as a flavoring agent in salad dressings or drizzled over vegetables or bread. There are many varieties available, so try a few and find your favorite. Some of them are milder and can be used in cooking.

PURE: Made from olives that have been heated and pressed to extract the last bit of oil. Pure oils are milder in flavor than extra-virgin. I often use them for sautéing because they don't overwhelm the dish.

olives

Olives come in many varieties, and each one has its own unique, bold, and salty flavor. They are a perfect addition to a chicken dish or pasta salad, but they also make a fantastic hors d'oeuvre. Buy a mix of different olives and set them out in separate bowls for your guests. Many grocery stores have olive bars, where you can find an assortment of olives in whatever quantity you would like. It is also great to have green olives on hand to complete your martinis.

BLACK OLIVES: Common black olives that come in cans are mild in flavor because they are not brined. They are versatile and are particularly good in pasta and orzo salads.

GREEN OLIVES: These olives are green because they are picked before they have had a chance to ripen on the tree. They have a bright and bold flavor.

KALAMATA OLIVES: Large Greek black olives with a velvety, rich flavor. They are often preserved in wine, olive oil, or vinegar. Look for pitted ones.

panko

These Japanese-style bread crumbs are larger and coarser than Western-style bread crumbs and are actually dried, toasted flakes of bread. Panko is available in Asian markets and supermarkets.

pepper

BLACK PEPPER: Always use freshly ground black peppercorns when a recipe calls for black pepper.

WHITE PEPPER: I use freshly ground white peppercorns, especially with light-colored sauces. White peppercorns are picked after they have ripened and have a tamer flavor than black peppercorns.

peppermint extract

Peppermint extract is good in hot chocolate and in chocolate desserts, particularly during the holidays.

pomegranate juice

Buy bottled sweetened pomegranate juice, which you'll find in the refrigerator case of your market. It is excellent in beverages, salad dressings, and marinades.

port

Use a tawny port for cooking. Aged and slightly sweet, with woodsy and caramel flavors, tawny port enhances sauces. It is particularly good with mushrooms.

potatoes

Potatoes are a great party food because there are so many different kinds, and they are really easy to make for crowds. If you are leaving the skin on, make sure you scrub your potatoes really well.

FINGERLINGS OR BABY DUTCH POTATOES: These make a perfect, simple side dish and are a great crowd-pleaser. Toss them with olive oil, salt and pepper, and any other seasonings you like and roast them.

RED AND WHITE POTATOES: Great roasting potatoes, and they are perfect for adding body and texture to stews and soups.

RUSSETS: Great for baking or for the perfect backyard grilled potato salad.

SWEET POTATOES: They have yellow or orange flesh. The orange-flesh potatoes are sometimes referred to as garnet yams.

YELLOW FINN AND YUKON GOLD: When mashed, these potatoes are creamy and smooth, but use them any way you like. They are my go-to, all-purpose potato.

preserved meats

These may be the star ingredients at your party. They are great for parties because they are so versatile— use them in appetizers and entrées.

APPLEWOOD-SMOKED BACON: Lightly smoked, this tastes good with most dishes calling for bacon.

PANCETTA: This is a type of bacon from the belly. It is salted, lightly spiced, and then cured rather than smoked. You can get it from the deli counter cubed or sliced, thick or thin. American bacon may be substituted if necessary.

PROSCIUTTO: Dry-cured ham that is thinly sliced for you at the deli counter. Select the imported Italian brand or the domestic artisan variety. Try wrapping fresh fruits and cheeses with prosciutto for an elegant hors d'oeuvre. Keep refrigerated.

TURKEY AND CHICKEN SAUSAGES: Found in most grocery stores now, these lighter options to traditional pork sausage still pack tons of flavor. Try chicken chorizo with Mexican dishes, or a ground Italian turkey sausage in pasta sauces or on pizza. Keep frozen until needed.

roasted peppers

Sweet roasted red or yellow bell peppers come in a jar packed in water, chopped or whole. Rinse and drain them well before using. They're good in appetizers, sauces, pasta dishes, and eggs.

sake

This Japanese wine is made from fermented rice and water. Its unusual flavor works especially well in marinades. Look for an inexpensive variety with an alcohol content of between 10 and 20 percent.

salt

I like fine-grained sea salt and kosher salt because they taste better than regular iodized table salt. I use Maldon sea salt, from Essex, England, because its flakes dissolve in food better than granules do. Just crumble it with your fingers to add while you are cooking. The salt has a distinctly sweet, yet mild, briny flavor that makes everything tastes better.

seriously simple seasoning salt

A combination of spices, herbs, garlic, and salt, this magical seasoning mix enhances the flavor of just about any savory dish. Use it as a rub and in vegetables, stews, and soups. See recipe on page 217.

sesame oil

All you need is a drop to add really bold sesame flavor to dressings and sauces. Store in a dark place.

sesame seeds

Sesame seeds come white or black. They are great for making a crust on meats and fish and for garnishing. Toast them over medium heat in a dry pan to bring out their flavor. Or look for toasted sesame seeds in the spices section of your supermarket.

shredded coconut

SWEETENED SHREDDED COCONUT: Use this when you want a sweet coconut flavor and for toasting and garnishing desserts.

UNSWEETENED SHREDDED COCONUT: This has a more pronounced coconut flavor than the sweetened variety and makes a great topping for sweet potatoes or squash.

sour cream and crème fraîche

I keep both of these in my refrigerator to use in sauces and as a garnish. You can substitute light sour cream in many dishes.

soy sauce

Use the light variety as it has less sodium. Not just delicious in Asian cooking, soy sauce can be the perfect salty addition to dressings, marinades, and sauces.

spices and dried herbs

Spices have about a six-month shelf life. Just a small amount of these basics can add huge flavor to your party dishes. Keep your pantry stocked with cayenne pepper, red pepper flakes, chili powder, ground cinnamon, dried oregano, thyme, rosemary, whole nutmeg (for grating yourself), ground cumin, paprika, and smoked paprika for last-minute cooking.

sugar

Keep granulated sugar in the pantry for baking. You may also want to have ultra-fine baking sugar (sometimes called baker's sugar) on hand to use interchangeably with granulated sugar. Powdered sugar is useful for decorating desserts.

toffee bits

These come in bags in the baking section of the grocery store. They make a wonderful quick topping for ice cream and a tasty addition to baked goods like cookies, brownies, or bar cookies.

tomatoes

A sweet and bright tomato flavor can be added to many savory dishes. Fresh tomatoes are best used in season. I have found that hothouse tomatoes don't have as much flavor as a ripe summer or early fall tomato. Cherry tomatoes are a good alternative to hothouse tomatoes, while canned or bottled tomatoes can add great flavor at minimal cost.

CHERRY TOMATOES: You can find yellow and red cherry tomatoes year-round in many markets. The possibilities for using cherry tomatoes are endless. Brighten up a dish with both color and flavor by adding a combination of yellow and red ones. They make salads, soups, sides, and entrées pop. Cherry tomatoes also help minimize party stress because there is no chopping required for these bite-size gems.

CRUSHED AND DICED CANNED TOMATOES: Try when making sauces or soups. They have much of the sweetness of fresh tomatoes. Look for San Marzano tomatoes. Try a fire-roasted diced tomato to add a unique smoky flavor to your next tomato soup.

MARINARA SAUCE: We don't always have the time to make marinara sauce from scratch. There are many prepared marinara sauces available, so make sure you grab a good one. Check that the consistency is thick and does not seem to be diluted with water. My favorite is made from San Marzano tomatoes because they are picked at the height of ripeness.

SUN-DRIED TOMATO PASTE: Instead of using traditional tomato paste to thicken a sauce and add body, try sun-dried tomato paste and add some extra punch, too. You can buy it in a tube and keep it in your refrigerator. The paste has a highly concentrated tomato flavor with a bit more sweetness than traditional tomato paste.

vanilla extract

Buy only a bottle labeled "pure vanilla." I like the bold-flavored Tahitian pure vanilla, available in the gourmet section of your supermarket.

vegetable oil

I like to use canola for its high smoke point and clean flavor. Grapeseed oil is also good.

vinegar

Great for making homemade sauces, marinades, and vinaigrettes for any meal. Vinegars will keep well in your pantry, so have these on hand.

BALSAMIC: Deep in color and slightly thicker than other vinegars, balsamic makes a great vinaigrette or a marinade for chicken. Or use it to make Balsamic Syrup (page 206) to drizzle over salads, cheese, figs, or tomatoes. For cooking, buy a moderately priced balsamic vinegar.

RED WINE VINEGAR: Its full-bodied, classic vinegar flavor is perfect for making vinaigrettes.

RICE WINE VINEGAR: Gives sauces and dressings a mild and slightly sweet vinegar flavor. Rice wine vinegar is great in marinades with soy sauce and fresh herbs.

SHERRY VINEGAR: A little goes a long way with this bold and distinctive vinegar. Produced in Spain, good quality sherry vinegar adds an assertive flavor to vinaigrettes and sauces.

worcestershire sauce

This is always good to have on hand for punching up the flavor of a sauce.

party entertaining styles

Parties can range from large backyard potlucks and barbecues to an intimate dinner for two. Planning ahead for your party is the key to handling any size group with ease so you can enjoy yourself. Regardless of the type of party you are hosting, if the food is good and the atmosphere is festive, everyone will have a good time.

sit-down

Sit-down dinners are a formal type of party and are best planned for a small group—ideally between four and eight guests. This type of party allows you to control the portion size and arrange food attractively on each plate. When food is plated, the atmosphere tends to be calm because people aren't running back to a buffet or constantly asking for food to be passed. If you are looking for some uninterrupted conversation time, a sit-down meal may be your best choice. Serve an entrée that does not need to be carefully watched while cooking or that can sit for a while after it's done.

Think dishes like Roasted Halibut with Mint Pea Purée (page 125) or Sweet and Spicy Orange-Hoisin Chicken (page 132) or Pomegranate-Marinated Grilled Lamb Chops (page 149). Similarly, pick a dessert that can be made and even plated ahead of time, so you don't spend half of the meal in the kitchen. Puff pastry fruit tarts (see page 187) are one of my favorite desserts for sit-down dinners because they can be made year-round (the fruit will vary, depending upon what is in season). The fruit tarts look very elegant and can be reheated just before serving.

family-style

For casual parties at home, try a family-style dinner. Bring the food to the table in serving dishes and let your guests serve themselves. This is a great option if you think that some of your guests won't eat some dishes and will want more of others. Offering the food family-style will save you from having to plate each serving differently. Dishes like flatbreads (see page 111), Indian Summer Risotto (page 98), and Sautéed Chicken Breasts with Port Mushroom Sauce (page 133) lend themselves to this casual serving style. They all look bountiful and beautiful on platters and in bowls. You can even serve your drinks family-style by placing pitchers of water and wine bottles on the table so that guests take what they want during the meal.

A family-style dinner party can be casually elegant. Choose pretty serving dishes and serving utensils and arrange each food thoughtfully. Attractive bowls filled with salads and vegetables sparkle when lined up along the center of the dining table.

To make last-minute preparations easier on the day of the party, get out the serving dishes and utensils you will need a day ahead of time and label what they are for with sticky notes. Avoid platters that will be too large or heavy for your guests to pass around the table.

buffet

When you are expecting a large group for a party and your guests will be arriving at different times, a buffet is a great way to have food ready for them. It can also be a really simple way to entertain that keeps you, the host, out of the kitchen and able to enjoy the company of your friends and family.

Some dishes work especially well at a buffet. Salads, frittatas, whole fish, braised meat and chicken dishes, and puréed or roasted vegetables hold up well for a prolonged period of time. In the Menus section, you'll find some good choices for buffet entertaining, such as the Family and Friends Buffet Lunch Get-Together (page 34) and the Graduation, Wedding, or Shower Celebration Dinner (page 40).

A day or two ahead of the party, think about which platters, bowls, and serving utensils you will need and how and where you will set up the buffet. If you are anticipating a large group, try having separate tables for food and drinks to keep the lines moving. Caterers and party planners create height on their buffet tables by draping boxes with fabric or napkins. Another simple way to add an element of drama is to use cake stands at different heights to hold bowls and platters. A good buffet looks abundant and plentiful while leaving space for guests to navigate. To save yourself some stress, try inviting one or two of your creative guests to come early and arrange the buffet, so you just have to take care of the cooking.

potluck

Potluck-style parties are a great way to get your guests involved in dinner preparations while reducing the stress for you, the host. You come up with the concept of the party and provide a main dish or two and drinks. Then you determine what other types of dishes you would like, such as an appetizer, salad, side, pasta, and dessert. From there you discuss with your guests what to bring. You can assign them specific recipes or let each person choose a dish. If your guests are choosing, you'll want to make sure that you're going to end up with a balanced meal, from appetizers to dessert. You don't want three lasagnas, a chocolate cake, and no vegetables!

If your main dish is an ethnic one, you can make the country of origin a theme and ask your guests to prepare dishes from that country. For example, if you were planning to make Oven-Baked Paella (121), you could encourage your guests to bring Spanish dishes. If a guest is anxious about cooking, suggest an easy recipe or ask him or her to pick up a dessert from a bakery or a bottle of wine.

outdoors

I am partial to outdoor parties when the weather cooperates. Nothing is more relaxing than enjoying a meal outdoors. Whether it is a dinner before an outdoor concert; a casual picnic on a boat, at a park, or at the beach; or a dinner on my patio, I choose dishes that do well in an outdoor setting. These include food with vinaigrette sauces, vegetable salads with vinaigrette dressings, vegetables in general, and fruit desserts without creams or custards.

If you are planning to host an outdoor party away from your home, at least one good ice chest or cooler is essential. There's such a large variety available today that you can choose one that will meet your particular needs. If you're planning a picnic party for a large group, you may want to invest in coolers in different sizes to accommodate the assorted shapes of various food containers. It's also helpful to be able to separate the cold dishes from the warm ones. Packets of frozen reusable ice packs in different sizes will keep food chilled for three to four hours.

PACKING AND SERVING YOUR PICNIC: Packing and serving food for a picnic requires careful planning. These tips should help you organize so that your food arrives as fresh as it was when it left the kitchen.

- Pack the foods to be eaten last at the bottom of the bag or chest, and the foods that will be eaten first on top. That way you won't have to unpack everything at once.
- Use vacuum-sealed containers to avoid leaks and soggy bags. For extra reinforcement, tape the lids with masking tape. Put the containers in lock-top plastic bags.
- Pack soft foods like deviled eggs, soft cheeses, tomatoes, and fruit in hard plastic containers or egg cartons.
- If you are serving a hot soup, preheat the thermos with boiling water. For a cold soup, chill the thermos with ice water for several minutes.
- Divide or cut the portions in your kitchen. It's much easier to serve pieces or slices of grilled chicken or fish than to carve them outside.

AN OUTDOOR PARTY AT YOUR HOME: Any of the previous styles of parties can be translated into an outdoor party at your home. The key to a successful outdoor party is utilizing your outdoor space. If you have a grill, use it to make a few dishes on your menu so you can spend time outside with your guests. If it is warm outside, keep your waters, soft drinks, wines, and juices on ice so they will stay cold throughout the evening. Dishes that need to be refrigerated until serving can be stored in a large cooler with ice and kept in the cooler so you have everything at the ready. Keep in mind that when you are outside, you may have to deal with nature. Clip down your tablecloths with large clips so they don't blow in the wind, and have citronella candles on hand in case there are bugs.

stocking the bar

These are the items that I find useful to have on hand for cocktails and other beverages:

glassware

I prefer to have a variety of simple, versatile glassware that can be used for any type of drink. Don't be afraid to use wine goblets for most of your drinks if that is all you have. Check out your local housewares store, which will often have packages of twelve of a kind for a reasonable cost. And remember, if you are having a big party, you can always rent the glasses. When I rent I order flutes and all-purpose wine goblets.

I keep four types of glasses on hand:
- All-purpose wine glasses (10 to 12 ounces)
- Fluted champagne glasses for all sparkling wine
- Martini glasses
- Old-fashioned (6-ounce) glasses

I also like to buy wine tags to mark each wine glass and avoid mix-ups.

other must-have tools

- Corkscrew
- Drink measurer
- Ice bucket and tongs
- Martini shaker and strainer
- Muddler
- Seasonal cocktail napkins
- Shot glass
- Small wooden board and knife for cutting garnishes

tips for serving wine and other beverages

Here are some easy tips to ensure that you will always be ready for a party.

- Create a separate beverage center. To prevent uncomfortable bottlenecks, choose a place away from the food that will allow for easy traffic flow. Remember that you can also serve hot drinks like coffee and tea at the beverage center.
- Make sure to have enough ice. Have an ice bucket with tongs for a small party. For a larger one, use a cooler to store extra ice. A cooler is also a great place to arrange a variety of soft drinks or beer on ice for a more casual gathering. Look for pretty galvanized steel coolers.
- I love to serve a signature cocktail when my guests arrive. It gets the party going, and it also cuts down on bartending. See the Beverages chapter for some fun examples. To make your party planning simpler, stick to one or two drinks for your party so you can enjoy time with your guests instead of serving as a bartender.
- If you're expecting wine lovers, you don't have to be an expert or spend hours looking for the right wines for your party. Visit a wine shop and ask for a recommendation within your price range, based on your menu. The staff can help you find wines that will complement it perfectly.
- Beer can be a refreshing choice, especially for outdoor summer parties. Again, ask an expert at your liquor store for recommendations to fit your menu.

beverages and spirits to have on hand

BEER: When serving beer at a party, stock both light and regular beer so everyone will be happy. I always think about the crowd I am serving. For serious beer lovers, select some unusual craft beers. And for more casual parties, look for your favorite football party brew. You can also try something a little different while supporting your community: Check out some local breweries near you and select regional brews for your next party.

CHAMPAGNE: The ultimate celebratory drink. With a little Champagne, dressing up a simple party is easy. True Champagne comes only from the Champagne region in France. It's expensive, so save it for special occasions. Make sure the Champagne is chilled, and have proper tulip-shaped champagne glasses for it.

COFFEE AND TEA: Your guests may like coffee or tea with dessert or brunch. It is a good idea to keep both caffeinated and decaffeinated coffee and tea on hand.

With tea, it is nice to have at least one herbal, black, and green tea available. Peppermint tea is a great after-dinner drink because it helps with digestion. You can use all-purpose mugs. Don't forget to put out cream and sweeteners.

LIQUEUR: Liqueurs come in fruit, spice, coffee, chocolate, and herbal flavors. There are hundreds of varieties. Try using a liqueur to make a mixed drink that will pick up on the seasonal flavors in your menu. Fruity liqueurs can be added to fruit sauces as toppings for cakes or other desserts.

A few of my favorites:

Cointreau: A light, orange-flavored liqueur, which is not too sweet and is good for both cooking and drinking.

Limoncello: An Italian lemon liqueur. Perfect mixed with sparkling wine and fresh fruit like blueberries for spring and summer cocktails, and also for light dessert sauces like zabaglione.

HOW MANY BOTTLES WILL YOU NEED?

Beverage	Bottle Size	Number Servings
BEER	12 ounces	1
SPARKLING WATER	1 liter	4
SPARKLING WINE	750 ml	6
SPIRITS	1 liter	22 cocktails, at 1½ ounces per drink
WINE	750 ml	5

Number Guests	White Wine	Red Wine	Sparkling Wine	Sparkling Water	Beer
6–8	2 bottles	2 bottles	1 bottle	2 bottles	8 bottles /cans
10–16	3 bottles	4 bottles	2 bottles	5 bottles	16 bottles/ cans
20	4 bottles	6 bottles	3 bottles	7 bottles	20 bottles/ cans

The table above left shows you how many servings per bottle of alcoholic beverage. The one above right will help you figure out what to have on hand. If you know your guests love red or white wine or beer, consider that when making your selection. And consider the menu, too. You don't have to offer all of the suggested beverages. You can make it Seriously Simple by limiting the variety. I always make sure to have extra wine and water on hand, just in case.

Peach liqueur: I use Mathilde, which is also from France. Great on fresh peaches or as a flavoring in drinks or sparkling wine.

St-Germain: Made from elderflowers, this French liqueur makes a delicious addition to cocktails and fruit desserts.

SPARKLING WATER: Sparking water is always great to have in your bar for guests. Make sure it is chilled. You can also combine it with fruit nectars and juices for homemade sparkling sodas (see the sidebar on page 49).

WINE: I always try to have at least one white and one red wine for my guests. If your guests will drink both, serve white wine with appetizers and salad and red wine with the main entrée. Or you can offer either one to your guests when they arrive.

Red wine: Most red wines should be stored and served a little cooler than room temperature, at between 60 and 65°F.

Rosé wine: These are excellent to serve at summer parties for their dry, yet slightly fruity flavor. They should be stored at 45 to 50°F.

Sparkling Wine: These varieties are an economical alternative to Champagne. I like serving Prosecco or cava when I am mixing a sparkling wine with other flavors like fruit juice or fruit liqueurs.

White wine: To maximize the flavor of white wine, store and serve it at 50 to 55°F.

party essentials

Following are a few tools and other items that will make cooking for and hosting your party easier.

digital timer

When you are cooking for a party, you may have several dishes cooking, baking, and grilling or broiling, all at the same time. A portable digital timer can time multiple tasks at once, so that every dish comes our perfectly cooked.

This gadget is especially helpful when you are cooking on an outdoor grill and have other things cooking inside. You can stay outside and still know when your food inside will be done. With a digital timer, you can make better use of your time because you can take care of other party tasks around the house without worrying about whether you will hear the kitchen timer go off. The digital timer is both a time-saver and a stress reliever!

immersion blender

An immersion blender, sometimes called a hand or a stick blender, is a perfect party tool because it makes for quick work and easy cleanup. It's ideal for making soups, sauces, salad dressings, smoothies, and drinks. The blender is simply a long stick with a rotary blade at the bottom, which can go directly into a pot or bowl, eliminating the need to transfer mixtures to a standing blender. And you don't have to wait for hot soups and sauces to cool before blending them.

For a refreshing summer smoothie, try combining fresh fruit, ice, milk, and agave syrup in a pitcher and simply blend with the immersion blender.

instant-read thermometer

You don't want to have to cut into your meat to check if it is done before serving it to guests, and you definitely don't want to serve them undercooked chicken or pork. So a reliable instant-read thermometer is a must for party cooking. It is a good idea to buy a thermometer that shows you doneness temperatures for various meats to eliminate any guessing.

large glass clamp jars

These are handy for storing sauces in the refrigerator.

lock-top plastic bags

I keep large and jumbo sizes. They're useful for marinating meat and for storage.

microplane zester

This great tool enables you to zest citrus and grate garlic or ginger very finely, so that your guests won't bite into big chunks of garlic or citrus zest.

The zester is very sharp, so be careful with your fingertips and knuckles while grating. When zesting citrus, grate only the colorful part of the skin, as the white pith underneath can be very bitter.

slow cooker

A slow cooker is handy for keeping moist dishes like stews or braises warm. Make sure to set it on low so the food will not overcook.

tongs

I use these in various sizes for turning foods in hot pans and for sautéing.

setting the table

Arranging a pretty table for your party is easy. The following suggestions will help you find your own Seriously Simple style.

candles

Candles are an easy way to decorate a table and create an intimate, warm mood. Be sure to use unscented candles so they don't compete with the aromas of the food. Small votives placed around the table can accentuate a centerpiece for a casual dinner. I like taller candles in candlesticks and candelabras for a more formal setting.

flowers and centerpieces

Simplicity is beautiful, so go for flowers that can be bought in bunches at the farmers' market. One or two dozen tulips in a vase is stunning. Small low, colorful bowls filled with baby roses are also lovely. Avoid flowers with very strong scents or overly large arrangements that will block guests from seeing each other.

Fruit centerpieces are another way to liven up the buffet or dining room table. For the cooler months, try bowls of fruit such as lemons, pomegranates, or clementines, and add some lemon leaves for greenery if you can find them. For spring and summer, try peaches, apricots, or plums. Bowls filled with colorful sweet bell peppers are another option.

serving pieces

Make sure that you have plenty of tongs, large serving spoons and forks, cheese knives, and spreaders. These will come in handy for buffet or family-style parties. And don't forget a pie or cake cutter.

table linens

Though they serve as the backdrop, table linens are important. I find white or cream-colored tablecloths to be the most versatile. Then I add colorful napkins, bright runners, and attractive centerpieces, cutlery, and glasses to balance the colors and design. The other advantage to white tablecloths is they can be bleached if stained.

Cloth napkins can be used for lining baskets as well as for table settings. Don't be afraid to mix and match. There are also beautiful paper napkins available now, which are printed with a toile pattern or party theme to make the cleanup really easy.

tables and tableware

Renting table linens and dishes and the tables themselves is a Seriously Simple way to throw a big party without adding a lot of expense. The beauty of rentals is that after the party, the tablecloths and napkins can be rolled up, wine stains and all, and returned, along with the tables. The cutlery, glasses, and china usually need just a quick rinse.

white or cream-colored platters, serving bowls, and plates

It's worth investing in a collection of simple white platters, bowls, and plates for serving. Look for different sizes that will accommodate the recipes you will be presenting. White bowls always look pretty on the table and accentuate the colors of the food. If you will be serving sauces, pick up some small sauce bowls as well. You can find these pieces at cookware or restaurant supply stores as well as housewares stores.

menus

These menus are a starting point for you. They begin seasonally with autumn because that's when most people start entertaining again after a relaxing summer. There is also a group of menus for year-round parties (see page 43). Don't feel you need to make every dish on a menu. You can always add or subtract dishes or substitute a simpler dish when you are short on time.

autumn

AUTUMN PAELLA
PARTY FOR 8

Suggested Beverage:
Sangria (page 52)

Prosciutto-Wrapped Figs with Burrata & Port & Balsamic Syrup (page 65)

Tapas Platter (page 66)

White Gazpacho (page 76) or Arugula Salad with Roasted Grapes (page 87)

Oven-Baked Paella (page 121)

Limoncello Zabaglione with Fresh Berries (page 179)

If the weather is great, enjoy this festive party outdoors. Arrange the figs and tapas platters on a table with the sangria. You can serve the paella buffet-style. The soup or salad is optional, depending upon how much time you have and the number of guests you are expecting. This is a festive menu that even beginner party givers will be able to master.

FALL GET-TOGETHER
DINNER FOR 8

Suggested Beverage:
Zinfandel wine

Butter lettuce salad with Buttermilk Garden Herb Dressing (page 205)

Beef Brisket with Zinfandel & Dried Fruit (page 156)

Crispy Potato & Apple Pancakes (page 166) with Maple-Cinnamon Applesauce (page 214)

Sautéed Green Beans in Sake Brown Butter (page 160)

Chocolate Caramel Matzo Brittle (page 183) or another chocolate dessert

This menu can all be made ahead of time and frozen. That makes it really simple to host this get-together. If you freeze the pancakes, make sure to reheat them until they are very hot and crispy. Matzo brittle might seem odd for a fall dessert, but in fact it can be enjoyed year-round. It never fails to be a conversation starter. Keep in mind this is also a dinner you could prepare for the Passover holiday with just a few minor changes. Eliminate the potato pancakes and serve Roasted Herbed Fingerling Potatoes (page 164) instead.

INDIAN SUMMER
DINNER PARTY FOR 6

Suggested Beverage:
Pinot Noir wine

Prosciutto-Wrapped Figs with Burrata & Port & Balsamic Syrup (page 65)

Indian Summer Risotto (page 98)

Grilled Chicken with Green Bean, Sweet Pepper & Tomato Salad & Romesco Sauce (page 130)

Pomegranate & Orange Granita (page 180) with assorted biscotti

It's always hard to say goodbye to summer. This menu, which I like to serve at my annual party, makes it a little bit easier. It highlights some of the bounty of late summer: fresh, juicy figs; sweet bell peppers; and thin, bright green beans. The almonds in the romesco sauce bring all the flavors together. There is a double dose of peppers in this menu—in the risotto and in the chicken dish. If you prefer, you can replace the peppers in the risotto with tomatoes or mushrooms or both. Don't forget to make the granita a few days ahead.

FALL HARVEST PARTY FOR 8 TO 12

Suggested Beverage:
Dry Riesling, light Pinot Noir, Grenache, or Beaujolais Nouveau wine

Warm Sweet & Spicy Mixed Nuts (page 58)

Butterflied Dry-Brined Roast Turkey with Maple Butter (page 138)

Sweet Potato Purée with Coconut Milk (page 168)

Roasted Brussels Sprouts & Winter Squash (page 162)

Apple and pear cobbler (a variation on Summer Stone Fruit Cobbler, page 188)

Whether you decide to serve this menu for Thanksgiving or you just want to throw a harvest party, the combination of flavors is sure to satisfy everyone at your table. Dry-brining a butterflied turkey creates a richly flavored, juicy bird. I love the fact that you carve the turkey in the kitchen and present it on a big platter. The sweet potatoes have an exotic island flavor that tastes wonderful with the turkey. Remember, you can always pick up a seasonal holiday dessert if time is short.

CASUAL BRUNCH FOR 6

Suggested Beverage:
Mimosas or sparkling wine

Banana-Peach Smoothies (page 48)

Thyme & Gruyère Egg Puffs with Sautéed Cherry Tomato Relish (page 108)

Blueberry Streusel Buttermilk Coffee Cake (page 194)

Fruit salad with yogurt-honey sauce

Start off your guests with mimosas (a simple mix of sparkling wine or Champagne with orange juice) when they come through the door. When all have arrived, bake the egg puffs so you can serve them right out of the oven. I am partial to the yummy flavor combination of the warm cherry tomato relish and the thyme-scented Gruyère egg puffs. You can make the coffee cake a day ahead and whip up the smoothies as you sit down at the table. This is a satisfying weekend brunch.

EASY FAMILY DINNER FOR 6

Suggested Beverage:
Cold sake

Grilled Sea Bass with Basil-Mint Sauce (page 124)

Sautéed Green Beans in Sake Brown Butter (page 160)

Israeli Couscous with Caramelized Leeks, Carrots & Zucchini (page 174)

Chocolate-Peppermint Pots de Crème (page 182)

Here's an easy dinner that you can serve anytime in late fall, whenever your family finds the time to sit down together. The sea bass is moist and tender and is greatly enhanced by the basil-mint sauce. The green beans take on a slightly nutty taste, and the couscous soaks up the other flavors. The chocolate-peppermint dessert is a traditional nod to the holidays.

winter

FAMILY AND FRIENDS BUFFET LUNCH GET-TOGETHER FOR 12 TO 16

Suggested Beverage:
Pinot Noir or Syrah wine

Butterflied Dry-Brined Roast Turkey Platter with Maple Butter (page 138), cold

Quinoa Salad with Pomegranates & Persimmons (page 93)

Cabbage & Apple Slaw with Agave-Citrus Dressing (page 83)

Assorted condiments and breads

Assorted seasonal fruits

Assorted bar cookies

Do you want to have a relaxed party where you don't spend a lot of time in the kitchen? This is the menu for you. It's my go-to afternoon spread when I know a big group of people will be coming and going. So much of this can be made in advance. The turkey should be chilled and the salads and condiments can be prepared a day ahead. To save time, you can always pick up a fruit platter from the market and assorted cookies and interesting breads from your favorite bakery.

HOLIDAY COCKTAIL PARTY FOR 12 TO 24

Suggested Beverage:
Sparkling Wine with Peach Nectar & Liqueur (page 53), plain sparkling wine, or a signature cocktail

Warm Sweet & Spicy Mixed Nuts (page 58)

Hawaiian Ahi Dip (page 62) with sesame crackers

Edamame Pesto Crostini (see page 86)

Crudités platter (see facing page)

Roasted Shrimp Cocktail with Mango Cocktail Sauce (page 68)

Grilled Chicken Skewers with Yogurt-Mango Curry Sauce (page 71)

Mini-Corn & Crab Cakes with Grilled Tomato Aioli (page 67)

Cheese platter (see page 42) with assorted toasts and sweet fruit condiments

You can make as many of these nibbles as time permits. Check the recipes to see what you can do way ahead of time, and then make a list of what needs to be done the day of the party. I always order a crudités platter to make the menu go farther. You may want to enlist a friend to make some of the dishes with you. The cheese platter with sweet fruit condiments adds an elegant finish to the menu.

NEW YEAR'S DAY OPEN HOUSE BRUNCH FOR 8

Suggested Beverage:
A sparkling cocktail

Deli Frittata (page 107)

Fruit salad with yogurt-honey sauce

Doughnut Muffins (page 184)

Cheese platter (see page 42) with assorted breads

This menu is perfect when you're expecting a small group to drop by for a low-key afternoon. The frittata is best made ahead and served room temperature. You can make up the batter for the muffins and finish them when your guests arrive. And you can even have your guests help you dip them in the cinnamon-sugar coating.

SUPER BOWL SUNDAY LUNCH FOR 10 TO 16

Suggested Beverage:
Craft beer

Warm Sweet & Spicy Mixed Nuts (page 58)

Chicken Drumettes with Romesco Sauce (page 72)

Parmesan-Artichoke Dip (page 61), crisp flatbread, and sliced carrots and celery

Meatball Sliders with Tomato Sauce (page 151) on Parmesan rolls

"The Wedge" with Blue Cheese Dressing, Pancetta & Cherry Tomatoes (page 84)

Brownie Toffee Cookies (page 199) or store-bought mini-cupcakes

When I make this lunch, I like to prepare everything but the salad ahead of time. You can rewarm the nuts, drumettes, and meatballs when you are ready to serve. It's hard to guess how many sliders will be consumed, but figure two to three per person. Put out the nuts, drumettes, and dip for the first half of the game. At halftime put the sliders and salad on a table and serve buffet-style. Be sure to provide plenty of napkins.

CRUDITÉS

Here's a list of raw and blanched vegetables that you can choose from to fill your basket or platter. Allow about 1/8 pound of each per person if you are serving a large variety of vegetables. Arrange the vegetables in neat stacks for a pretty presentation. Use a rectangular or circular platter or a decorative basket lined with red leaf lettuce.

- You can make the components of this platter up to 1 day ahead of time. Store the vegetables in separate lock-top plastic bags.

- If you're blanching vegetables, it's best to do so the morning of the party. Immerse the vegetables in a pot of boiling salted water for about 1 minute. Then drain and chill. When you're ready to serve, arrange the veggies on a platter with a bowl of the desired sauce.

- Here's a fun way to serve the crudités: Present the vegetables in martini or French jelly glasses of assorted heights (one type of veggie per glass). Arrange the glasses on a platter with microgreens placed around the bases of the glasses.

Vegetables for Serving Raw

- Green, purple, red, or yellow bell peppers, seeded and cut into strips
- Carrots, peeled and cut into sticks
- Celery, peeled and cut into sticks
- Sugar snap peas, strings removed, left whole
- Chinese snow peas, strings removed, left whole
- European cucumber, unpeeled and cut into sticks
- Jicama, peeled and cut into sticks
- Button mushrooms
- White and red radishes, trimmed
- Red and yellow cherry and pear tomatoes

Vegetables That Require Blanching

- Baby asparagus spears, tough bottom stalk removed
- French green beans, ends removed, left whole
- Broccoli, cut into florets

Sauces for Dipping

- Grilled Tomato Aioli (page 210)
- Buttermilk Garden Herb Dressing (page 205)
- Romesco Sauce (page 213)
- Tapenade mayonnaise (stir 1 tablespoon of tapenade into 1/2 cup of mayonnaise)

DOUBLING RECIPES

Doubling recipes can be tricky. Here are some tips to keep in mind:

- When baking, make the recipe twice rather than doubling it. Baking recipes often don't multiply successfully. By repeating the recipe, you are sure to have excellent results.

- As a rule, when you are doubling a sauce, soup, or marinade recipe, you only need one and a half times the amount of liquid called for.

- Instead of doubling seasonings, such as herbs and spices, multiply them by one and a half to begin with. Seasonings intensify when multiplied. Taste the dish for proper balance and add salt and pepper.

- If you can, use two pans of the recommended size. That way the dishes will finish cooking at the same time. When baking, if you change the depth of the pan, it will change the baking time.

- When baking or roasting with multiple pans, make sure to switch the pans midway through the baking time for even results. You may find the food takes a few more minutes to bake or roast because there is less air circulating with more than one pan in the oven. This is why having a visual cue for doneness or an oven thermometer is helpful.

- If you have two or more pans in the oven, you may also need to raise the temperature by 25°F.

SOUPS-ON WARM-UP DINNER FOR 8

Suggested Beverage:
Grenache or Rhône wine

Mixed winter greens with Roasted Shallot & Garlic Vinaigrette (page 87)

Turkey Vegetable Soup with Pesto (page 82) or Steamed Mussels with Garlic, Tomatoes & Fresh Herbs (page 116)

Herbed Garlic Cheese Bread (page 59)

Chocolate-Peppermint Pots de Crème (page 182) and/or your favorite brownies

It's cold and rainy, or maybe even snowing. What could be better than a comforting bowl of soup or steamed mussels along with toasted cheesy garlic bread to soak up the juices? A simple salad begins the dinner and smooth, chocolatey pots de crème or a big plate of brownies makes the perfect ending.

VALENTINE'S DAY DINNER FOR 6

Suggested Beverage:
Sparkling Wine with Peach Nectar &
Liqueur (page 53), sparkling wine, or
Champagne

**Smoked Salmon with Crispy Shallots
& Dilled Cream (page 70)**

**Crispy Duck Breast with Cherry Port
Sauce (page 141)**

**Penne with Roasted Broccoli &
Pistachio Gremolata (page 104)**

**Shortbread with Chocolate &
Candied Walnuts (page 200)**

Sometimes I prepare this menu
for my husband and myself, but
other times I like to invite over a
group to celebrate friendship with
a bit of romance. You can multiply
or reduce the recipes easily. Since
the menu is streamlined, I prefer
to serve it as a sit-down dinner.
Golden brown, crispy shallot rings
adorn the smoked salmon. Salty
and sweet and slightly creamy,
this is the appetizer to serve for
romantic or special dinners. The
duck breasts cook quickly, as does
the delicious sauce. The sweet
and crumbly cookies are a lovely
way to end the evening, along with
espresso or your favorite coffee.

ACADEMY AWARDS POTLUCK PARTY FOR 6 TO 8

Suggested Beverage:
Red Carpet Cocktail (page 48) and
full-boded Zinfandel or Cabernet
Sauvignon wine

**Warm Sweet & Spicy Mixed Nuts
(page 58)**

Crudités platter (see page 35)

**Store-bought hummus and tzatziki
with pita crisps**

**Mixed Greens with Edamame Pesto
Crostini (page 86)**

**Baked Greek Pasta (page 102)
or Spicy Mac and Cheese with
Caramelized Leeks (page 100)**

**Puff Pastry Almond Fruit Tarts
(page 187) or store-bought tart**

What's more fun than getting a
group of friends together to watch
the awards? I let my guests choose
whether to bring an appetizer, salad,
or dessert, while I make the main
course. Put out an array of appetizers
for your guests to munch on, along
with a signature cocktail, while you
are watching the preshow. As the
evening progresses, you can heat
the pasta. Put the salad and pasta
on a buffet table with large plates
and forks and napkins for your
guests, so they can balance the
dish on their laps while watching
the show.

SUNDAY NIGHT DINNER FOR 6

Suggested Beverage:
Malbec wine

**Baby Spinach Salad with Winter
Squash & Bacon (page 90)**

**Braised Chicken Thighs with Red
Wine & Wild Mushrooms (page 136)**

**Israeli Couscous with Caramelized
Leeks, Carrots & Zucchini (page 174)**

**Caramel Coconut Ice-Cream Terrine
or Chocolate Caramel Matzo Brittle
(page 181 or 183)**

This is one of those menus I never
tire of serving. It's comforting
and inviting on a chilly night.
Roasted, slightly caramelized
winter squash and crispy bacon
accent the baby spinach salad.
Reminiscent of coq au vin, the
chicken thighs pair beautifully
with the tasty yet neutral couscous.
Make sure to plan ahead as the
terrine or matzo brittle needs to
be made in advance.

spring

Here's a savory brunch that highlights spring's bounty of asparagus, peas, rhubarb, and strawberries. The lemony spritzer is light and refreshing and perfect as an early afternoon cocktail. Choose some pretty, small glass bowls for serving the chilled cucumber and pea soup, which begins the meal. The crustless quiche is lighter than its crusted cousin, and the sweet-and-salty bacon offers a crispy textural contrast. And for dessert a crostata, a country-style one-crust pie, is bursting with big fruity flavor.

WEEKDAY DINNER PARTY FOR 4 TO 6

Suggested Beverage:
Cabernet Sauvignon wine

Pomegranate-Marinated Grilled Lamb Chops (page 149)

Steamed spinach

Roasted Herbed Fingerling Potatoes (page 164)

Strawberries and blood oranges with Port & Balsamic Syrup (page 207) and assorted store-bought cookies

When I want to throw a casual weekday dinner party, I plan a menu of easy dishes that can be put together quickly. This is one of those menus. Look for young spring lamb chops. In the morning, toss them in the pomegranate-mint marinade, which goes beautifully with the lamb. Roast the potatoes and steam the spinach when you get home from work. A big bowl of ripe strawberries and blood orange sections takes little time to assemble. The syrup brings out the berries' sweetness.

MAKE YOUR OWN PIZZA OR FLATBREAD PARTY FOR 8

Suggested Beverage:
Grenache wine

Arugula Salad with Roasted Grapes (page 87)

Homemade Pizza Dough (page 113) or store-bought

Assorted pizza toppings (see page 112)

Assorted ice creams and sorbets

Who doesn't love pizza? Here's a casual party where you can make the pizzas with the suggested toppings or let everyone have a vote on his or her own additions. The pizza should be the star of the party. The arugula salad is all you need to accompany the pizzas. Depending upon the weather and your inclination, you can grill these outside or bake them in the oven. Put out an assortment of ice creams and sorbets for dessert for a simple ending to a fun party.

LAST-MINUTE DINNER PARTY FOR 6

Suggested Beverage:
Chardonnay or Sauvignon Blanc wine

"The Wedge" with Blue Cheese Dressing, Pancetta & Cherry Tomatoes (page 84)

Roasted Halibut with Mint Pea Purée (page 125)

Roasted Carrots (page 161)

Limoncello Zabaglione with Fresh Berries (page 179)

A crisp wedge of iceberg lettuce topped with tasty garnishes is so easy to put together and is always enjoyed. For a main course, pick any fish fillet you like; salmon and sea bass are also good in this dish. I like to make the zabaglione in the morning and chill it to serve as a topping on the berries.

summer

OUTDOOR CONCERT DINNER FOR 6

Suggested Beverage:
Sparkling wine and Sauvignon Blanc

Grilled Artichoke Halves with Grilled Tomato Aioli (page 63)

Chilled Buttermilk Corn Soup (page 77)

Grilled Chicken Breasts with Herbed Green Sauce (page 134)

Orzo Vegetable Salad (page 94)

Brownie Toffee Cookies (page 199)

Fresh cherries and white peaches or nectarines

For me, the summer starts the night the Hollywood Bowl opens. It's a leisurely evening with plenty of time to enjoy a few courses before the concert starts. I pack everything in reusable containers and make sure to have ice packs in each insulated bag. The meal begins with grilled artichokes and sparkling wine. The corn soup is poured from a chilled thermos into pretty bowls. The grilled chicken and colorful orzo salad make a satisfying main course, which is excellent at room temperature. Don't forget extra napkins, garbage bags, silverware, unbreakable glassware, reusable plastic or bamboo bowls and plates, and a corkscrew.

MEXICAN FIESTA FOR 6

Suggested Beverage:
Sangria (page 52)

White Gazpacho (page 76)

Mexican Seafood & Scallion Sauté with Mango-Avocado Salsa (page 118)

Black Beans with Chorizo & Chipotle Cream (page 172)

Warm corn and flour tortillas

Caramel Coconut Ice-Cream Terrine (page 181)

For the main course, scallops and shrimp are flavored with a Mexican-style marinade of tequila and lime juice. You can prepare the gazpacho, beans, and ice-cream terrine a few days ahead. Then the only thing you will have to cook at the last minute is the seafood. To serve, arrange the seafood on a platter and the beans and the salsa in separate bowls. Make sure to have a pitcher of sangria to serve with the meal.

GRADUATION, WEDDING, OR SHOWER CELEBRATION DINNER FOR 12

Suggested Beverage:
White Wine Frozen Fruit Spritzer (page 51) or Zinfandel or Syrah wine

Tapas Platter (page 66)

Prosciutto-Wrapped Figs with Burrata & Port & Balsamic Syrup (page 65)

Mixed Greens with Edamame Pesto Crostini (see page 86)

Grilled Tri-tip of Beef with Herb Rub (page 155)

Grilled Sweet Peppers, Eggplant & Corn (page 171)

Summer Stone Fruit Cobbler (page 188) with French vanilla ice cream

Big dinner parties require a strategy to help the cook/host have a successful outcome. Enlist a friend who enjoys grilling to take charge of the task. You can prepare the appetizers hours ahead. The dessert can be made in the morning and reheated before serving. Offer glasses of the frozen fruit spritzer as guests arrive. Arrange the appetizers close to the beverage center, and make sure to have little plates, forks, and cocktail napkins nearby. A shallow salad bowl with the crostini adds to the beautiful presentation.

FOURTH OF JULY PARTY FOR 8 TO 16

Suggested Beverage:
Craft beer or Grenache wine

Assorted dips and crudités platter (see page 35)

Pulled Pork (page 144) with Hawaiian bread buns

Sweet Corn Pudding (page 169)

Summer Caprese Salad with Watermelon, Cucumber & Feta Relish (page 88)

Summer Stone Fruit Cobbler (page 188)

If I am having a big crowd, I sometimes ask my guests to bring a dish. You could ask yours to bring the dips and crudités, or the cobbler or a summer dessert of their choice. The pulled pork can be made days ahead of time. Arrange the sandwiches on a big platter. The creamy sweet corn pudding and the colorful reinterpretation of a caprese salad will look pretty laid out on a buffet table beside the sandwiches. Have plates, napkins, and forks at one side of the table for your guests to pick up and serve themselves.

BEACH PICNIC FOR 6

Suggested Beverage:
Lemonade and iced tea

Italian Picnic Sandwich (page 109)

Cabbage and Apple Slaw with Agave-Citrus Dressing (page 83)

Fresh apricots, peaches, and nectarines

Shortbread with Chocolate & Candied Walnuts (page 200)

A big blanket spread out on the sand, this menu, and some good friends are the ingredients for a memorable afternoon at the beach. It's also fun to set up at the end of the day and watch the sun go down. You might want to include a bottle of sparkling wine, if your locality permits it. Don't forget to pack the food in coolers. Be creative with the picnic sandwiches and use fillings that you love. The cookies should be stored in a cooler so the chocolate doesn't melt.

BACKYARD BARBECUE FOR 6 TO 8

Suggested Beverage:
Rosé wine or Sangria (page 52)

The Perfect Burger (page 154)

Ahi Burgers with Ginger-Sesame Mayonnaise (page 123)

Assorted relish tray with lettuce, tomatoes, onions, and pickles

Potato Salad with Sun-Dried Tomato–Caper Vinaigrette (page 95)

Cabbage & Apple Slaw with Agave-Citrus Dressing (page 83)

Strawberry Shortcake with White Chocolate Whipped Cream (page 192)

This laid-back menu celebrates summer. My idea of a perfect hamburger is made with freshly ground chuck or brisket (or a mix of the two), topped with caramelized onions and creamy blue cheese, and tucked into a toasted bun. For those who prefer fish, make the ahi (tuna) burgers. In fact the meat lovers may want to sign up for an ahi burger once they take a bite! The ginger-sesame mayonnaise adds just the right note. Strawberry shortcake with a dollop of white chocolate whipped cream will bring smiles all around.

CHEESE FOR ANY PARTY

A cheese course or platter can make a Seriously Simple addition to any party. With a few guidelines and tips, anyone can assemble a good selection of cheeses. Cheese plates are also a great way to set the tone of formality for a party.

Casual Parties
One large cheese platter that is ready for guests as they walk in creates a great focal point for people to gather around and converse before the meal is served. If you are still cooking, you can place this platter in or near the kitchen, to encourage your guests to participate in the preparation of the meal. You could also ask a guest to bring the cheese platter, making your work even simpler.

Buffet-Style Parties
For a buffet-style party, a cheese platter can be set out at the beginning with the appetizers and salads, or at the end, along with the dessert. Adding fruit, such as grapes, or a basket of bread to the cheese platter can bring a lot of visual appeal to your buffet.

Formal Parties
For an elegant way to wind down at the end of the meal, serve each guest a plate with small tastes of three or four cheeses instead of a dessert course. Arrange the cheeses on each plate from mildest to strongest, and encourage your guests to taste the cheeses in that order.

Like fruits and vegetables, different cheeses peak at various times of the year. It is a good idea to investigate which cheeses are at their best before your party. Here are a few ideas for cheeses and accompaniments for each season:

Spring
Pungent blue cheeses can brighten up springtime parties. Serve with fresh fruits, such as strawberries and grapes.

Summer
The tangy and bright flavors of fresh goat's and sheep's milk cheeses tend to marry nicely with summer dishes that include fruits, especially citrus. These cheeses tend to peak in the summer months. Firmer aged sheep's milk cheeses have a bolder and nuttier flavor, and they can also make a great addition to a summer party menu.

Autumn
Hard and nutty cheeses like Gruyère pair nicely with autumn flavors. Serve with fresh figs, pears, or dried fruits and roasted nuts to add warmth to any autumn party.

Winter
For a buffet or casual cheese platter, baked Brie is a comforting and hearty choice. Spread apricot jam on top of a wheel of Brie and bake at 325°F for 10 to 15 minutes to warm the cheese and melt the jam. Serve with sliced apples and a sliced quick bread containing fruit and nuts.

Here are a few other tips to keep in mind when adding a cheese plate or platter to your next party menu:

- Always serve your cheese at room temperature. Remove hard cheeses from the refrigerator about 1 hour before serving and soft cheeses about 30 minutes before serving.

- For a cheese platter, it is a nice touch to label each cheese so that your guests know exactly what they are tasting. Provide a separate knife for each cheese.

- Think about whom you have invited to your party. If you know your guests don't tend to like strong flavors, stick to milder cheeses. If some of your guests are more adventurous, add a really bold or rare cheese to try.

- For dessert, serve cheeses with fruit (fresh or dried), honey or agave syrup, or candied nuts, such as pecans or walnuts, to provide your guests with the sweetness they may enjoy at the end of a meal.

- If you buy your cheese from a cheese store, ask the person working there for recommendations for wine or food pairings with the cheeses you select.

- If you are planning a party with dishes from a certain region of the world, try to pick cheeses that come from the same area to stick with the theme of the menu.

mix & match

VEGETARIAN DINNER FOR 6

Suggested Beverage:
Pinot Noir wine

Arugula Salad with Roasted Grapes (page 87)

Crusty bread

Potato & Wild Mushroom Gratin with White Truffle Cheese (page 165) or Spicy Mac & Cheese with Caramelized Leeks (page 100)

Roasted Carrots (page 161)

Steamed spinach or Swiss chard

Pomegranate & Orange Granita (page 180) with assorted cookies

The stars of this menu are fresh vegetables that are available in the market year-round. White dinner plates will make a lovely canvas for the woodsy, creamy vegetable gratin or spicy mac and cheese; simply steamed greens; and bright orange carrots, flecked with bronze. This might be fun to serve to a group of people who are not vegetarians. (If you must, add a simple grilled chicken or fish for those who need their protein.)

BIRTHDAY DINNER FOR 8

Suggested Beverage:
Dry Riesling or Sauvignon Blanc wine

Mixed Greens with Edamame Pesto Crostini (page 86)

Sweet & Spicy Orange-Hoisin Chicken (page 132)

Israeli Couscous with Caramelized Leeks, Carrots & Zucchini (page 174)

Mocha Celebration Cake (page 196)

I have a friend for whom I make this menu every year for her birthday. It's simple yet full of vibrant flavors. She looks forward to this orange chicken and Israeli couscous with vegetables. The good news about the cake is that it is one large layer, which makes it easy to frost, and it can feed an army. Divide up what is left; give some to your guests and stash a big wedge in your freezer for a future fabulous last-minute dessert.

DINNER FOR SEAFOOD LOVERS FOR 6

Suggested Beverage:
Sauvignon Blanc wine

Mini-Corn & Crab Cakes with Grilled Tomato Aioli (page 67)

Mixed greens with Basic Vinaigrette (page 204)

Roasted Shrimp Scampi Provençal (page 117)

Penne with Roasted Broccoli & Pistachio Gremolata (page 104)

Pomegranate & Orange Granita (page 180)

Do you have friends who love seafood? I do. I like to acknowledge their seafood appreciation with a couple of dishes that are really special. The crab cakes are studded with corn nuggets and can be garnished with your favorite aioli. And for a spin on scampi, I love the rustic roasting pan full of Provençal-style shrimp. Instead of tons of butter, you'll find a light and zesty tomato sauce glazing the juicy roasted shellfish. You can make up the granita days ahead. It's a perfect finish for the seafood flavors.

BIRTHDAY OR SHOWER LUNCHEON FOR 12

Suggested Beverage:
White Wine Frozen Fruit Spritzer
(page 51)

Whole Slow-Roasted Salmon with Sweet Mustard-Dill Aioli (page 127)

Deli Frittata (page 107)

Orzo Vegetable Salad (page 94)

Green Bean, Sweet Pepper & Tomato Salad (page 91)

Warm French rolls with unsalted butter

Mocha Celebration Cake (page 196)

I have served this in the heat of the summer and the chill of the winter. The salmon is cooked to perfection by slow-roasting it, which lends a velvety texture to the flesh. My guests are always surprised that it is so moist, yet cooked through. I like to offer an egg dish as well, and the frittata is just the ticket. The accompanying salads offer a textural and visual contrast. This menu can be made a day ahead, refrigerated, and served at room temperature. Serve the dishes on a table or counter, placing each one at a different height, using pedestals or cake platters.

ANNIVERSARY DINNER PARTY FOR 6

Suggested Beverage:
Champagne, Pinot Noir wine

Smoked Salmon with Crispy Shallots & Dilled Cream (page 70)

Sautéed Chicken Breasts with Port Mushroom Sauce (page 133)

Roast Herbed Fingerling Potatoes (page 164)

Roasted Carrots (page 161)

Limoncello Zabaglione with Fresh Berries (page 179) or with seasonal sliced fruit, and crisp butter cookies

Prepare this for just yourself and your loved one (you'll have delish leftovers), or invite your most special friends to celebrate your anniversary. This is party food that makes you feel festive. Champagne is a given for an anniversary celebration, and a tray of these smoked salmon appetizers is the perfect accompaniment. You can cook the chicken in advance and reheat it just before serving. If you want the evening to go on, serve some small dessert glasses of limoncello with dessert.

BOOK GROUP GET-TOGETHER LUNCH OR DINNER FOR 6 TO 8

Suggested Beverage:
Chardonnay wine

Smoky Tomato Soup (page 81)

Arugula Salad with Roasted Grapes (page 87)

Warm French rolls or focaccia

Store-bought cupcakes

This casual meal is truly Seriously Simple, and it is equally good for lunch or dinner. The tomato soup can be served in glass mugs. Serve the salad as is or add roast chicken for a more substantial main course.

DESSERT PARTY FOR 12 TO 24

Suggested Beverage:
An assortment of after-dinner liqueurs, like Grand Marnier and Baileys; eau de vie; or Cognac

Cheese and fruit platter (see page 42) with assorted breads and crackers

Mocha Celebration Cake (page 196)

Puff Pastry Almond Fruit Tarts (page 187)

Shortbread with Chocolate & Candied Walnuts (page 200)

Blueberry Streusel Buttermilk Coffee Cake (page 194)

A dessert party is a fun and different way to get a group together. Everyone seems to like a sweet, and with this menu, your guests will have a wonderful variety to choose from. The cookies and celebration cake can be made a day ahead. I also like to have a fruit and cheese platter on hand with simple crackers, fruit-flavored quick breads, and a pot of honey for drizzling over the cheese. Present each dessert on a different dish, at a different height (use footed platters) for an elegant look. Have a large pot of decaf coffee and an array of teas for your guests to choose from.

beverages

banana-peach smoothie

Smoothies are a great way to start a breakfast or brunch. Frozen peaches and fresh bananas are blended into a frothy, slightly creamy fruit refresher. These need to be made just before serving; otherwise they will separate.

serves 6

Combine all the ingredients in a blender and blend until smooth. Pour into individual glasses and serve immediately.

3 medium ripe bananas

1 pound frozen peaches

1 cup ice

½ cup nonfat plain or Greek yogurt

2 cups milk

1 tablespoon honey

red carpet cocktail

Special events deserve special cocktails. This is the drink I serve for watching awards shows. It is always a hit. Elderflower liqueur, with its hints of passion fruit and grapefruit, is the elegant surprise ingredient. For the sparkling wine, use a moderately priced bottle, like Prosecco or cava.

serves 1

Pour the liqueur into a champagne flute. Slowly pour enough sparkling wine into the glass so that it's three-quarters full. Garnish with the twist of lemon and serve immediately.

1 ounce St-Germain (elderflower liqueur)

Chilled sparkling wine to top off the drink

Twist of lemon

lemon-blueberry spritzer

Light and citrusy, this is a good cocktail to serve in the afternoon or for a prolonged cocktail hour. It is festive, with its bubbly bite, and colorful, with blueberries hugging the bottom of the cocktail glass.

serves 6

In a glass pitcher, combine all the ingredients and stir to blend. Pour into champagne flutes and serve immediately.

One 750-ml bottle chilled Prosecco

1 cup chilled sparkling water

½ cup limoncello

¼ cup blueberries

HOMEMADE SPARKLING FRUIT-FLAVORED SODAS

Making your own sparkling fruit-flavored sodas can be Seriously Simple and it's a fantastic, fresh addition to a party. Here are a few suggestions:

• Garnish the sodas with fresh fruit and mint.

• Try using nectars, such as peach or guava, for a thicker and more concentrated fruit flavor. Mix equal parts nectar and sparkling water and pour over ice.

• Sparkling lemonade is a classic favorite. Combine equal parts freshly squeezed lemon juice and sparkling water, and add sugar or sugar substitute to taste. Garnish with a lemon twist. You can also flavor the lemonade with nectars.

• Look for seasonal fruit juices to use in sparkling sodas. For example, try blood orange or grapefruit juice in the winter. Mix equal parts juice and sparkling water.

white wine frozen fruit spritzer

This gorgeous, refreshing drink is as beautiful to look at as it is delicious for your guests to sip. It is a twist on sangria, but lighter on the alcohol and full of fruit flavor. Use a glass pitcher if possible. I like to serve this at a cocktail party or as a welcoming beverage for a lazy afternoon brunch. The sparkling water and juices make this an excellent choice for hot days when you are thirsty. Since there is less alcohol, your guests can drink up and you don't have to worry about any embarrassingly drunken moments.

serves 8 to 12

In a large glass pitcher, combine all of the liquid ingredients. With your fingers, crush the mint leaves and add them to the mixture. Add the ice and the fruit. Mix with a long-handled spoon to combine. Pour into pretty goblets to serve.

party prep

This should be made just before serving.

One 750-ml bottle chilled Viognier wine

3 cups sparkling water

1½ cups tangerine juice

1½ cups cranberry juice

8 to 10 fresh mint leaves

1½ cups crushed ice

12 thinly sliced oranges

12 frozen strawberries

THE CLEVER COOK COULD:

- Use Sauvignon Blanc, Fumé Blanc, or even a California rosé instead of the Viognier.

- Use different juices, like guava and pomegranate, or pineapple and mango.

sangria

Make sure to start this a day ahead so you can marinate the strawberries, oranges, and peach, and freeze the grapes. Lambrusco is a light sparkling Italian wine with a low-alcohol content. It is a refreshing base for this sangria.

serves 8 to 12

1 In a large nonreactive bowl, combine the gin, Cognac, and orange liqueur. Add the strawberries, orange slices, and peach slices (if using). Cover and marinate overnight in the refrigerator.

2 Place the grapes on a baking sheet and freeze for at least 4 hours. When frozen, put in a lock-top plastic bag and seal. If not using the grapes immediately, return to the freezer.

3 In a large glass pitcher, combine the Lambrusco and orange juice and stir to blend. With your fingers, crush the mint leaves and add them to the mixture. Add the ice and marinated fruit. Mix with a long spoon to combine. Drop a few grapes into each pretty goblet and then add the sangria. Arrange an orange slice on the rim of each glass and serve.

party prep
Marinate the sliced fruit 1 day ahead and freeze the grapes up to 1 week ahead.

2½ ounces gin

2½ ounces Cognac

2½ ounces orange liqueur

2 cups sliced strawberries

3 oranges, halved crosswise and thinly sliced, reserving 8 to 12 slices for garnish

1 white peach or nectarine, thinly sliced (optional)

40 grapes

One 750-ml bottle chilled red Lambrusco

2 cups orange or tangerine juice

8 to 10 fresh mint leaves

1½ cups crushed ice

sparkling wine
with peach nectar & liqueur

You can serve this year-round, but I particularly like to serve it in the warm summer and early fall months. The double dose of peachiness could make it your summer go-to drink. Since the nectar and liqueur give the drink a slightly sweet flavor, serve it with savory appetizers like olives, nuts, and smoked salmon.

serves 1

Combine the peach nectar and liqueur in a champagne flute. Slowly pour the sparkling wine into the flute to fill it three-quarters full. Serve immediately.

1 tablespoon peach nectar

½ ounce peach liqueur (I use Mathilde, from France)

Chilled sparkling wine to top off the drink (use a moderately priced bottle, like Prosecco or cava)

cc cooler

I discovered this fabulous cocktail at Waterloo and City, one of my favorite restaurants in Culver City (the name of the drink is an abbreviation). It is refreshing and potent. Cucumber and fresh mint add a cooling touch. Muddling (or bruising, but not crushing) the cucumber helps release the juice and essential oils. A muddler is a handy tool to tackle this task, but you can use a pestle or even an ordinary spoon in a pinch.

Try to estimate how many drinks you will be serving, and have containers of cucumber, lime juice, and mint ready to go. You can use a cocktail shaker if you prefer to make a batch. I make these individually and keep 1- and 2-ounce measures close by.

serves 1

2 tablespoons thin European cucumber strips (about 3 inches long)

Ice cubes

2 ounces vodka

1 ounce St-Germain (elderflower liqueur)

2 tablespoons fresh lime juice

3 fresh mint leaves, torn

Sparkling apple cider, sparkling wine, or sparkling water to top off the drink

1 Put the cucumber in a cocktail glass and muddle it by pressing firmly.

2 Add ice cubes to the glass and then pour in the vodka, liqueur, and lime juice. Add the mint leaves and stir to combine.

3 Top off the drink with the sparkling cider and serve.

opetizers

warm sweet & spicy mixed nuts

These nuts, adapted from a recipe in *The Union Square Cafe Cookbook,* are addictive. The nuts are toasted and then coated with a mixture of cayenne pepper, herbs, and brown sugar. It's best to serve these warm for maximum flavor. Offer them with drinks and watch them disappear.

serves 6 to 8

1 Preheat the oven to 350°F. Spread out the nuts on a baking sheet and toast until golden brown, about 10 minutes.

2 In a large bowl, combine the remaining ingredients. With a big wooden spoon, stir the nuts in the herb mixture, making sure the butter melts and moving the nuts around so they are evenly coated. Transfer to a pretty bowl and let sit for 5 minutes to crisp the nuts before serving.

1 pound raw unsalted mixed nuts (pecans, walnuts, Brazil nuts, cashews, peanuts, and hazelnuts)

1 tablespoon finely chopped fresh rosemary

2 teaspoons chopped fresh thyme

1/2 teaspoon cayenne pepper

2 teaspoons dark brown sugar

2 teaspoons sea salt (I like to use Maldon)

1 tablespoon unsalted butter, cut up

THE CLEVER COOK COULD:

Slice some seasonal fruit and arrange on a platter. Place a mound of the nuts in the center for a super-easy after-dinner or lunch treat.

herbed garlic cheese bread

This is the perfect accompaniment for many grilled dishes. The bread slices are also nice as a casual appetizer to serve your guests while they wait for dinner.

serves 8

1 Preheat the oven to 400°F. Combine the dip, thyme, and oregano in a small bowl. Blend well.

2 Cut the bread in half lengthwise, and spoon half the mixture on each half of the bread. Spread it out evenly with a spatula. Sprinkle the bread with the Parmesan cheese.

3 Cut the bread halves about three-quarters of the way through into 2-inch-thick slices. Make sure that you haven't cut all the way through, and the crust is still holding the bread together. Wrap each half tightly in aluminum foil.

4 Place the loaves on a baking sheet and bake for 10 to 15 minutes. Remove from the oven and remove the foil. Turn the oven to broil and put the bread under the broiler about 4 inches away from the heat for 1 to 2 minutes, or until nicely browned. Place on a platter or in a napkin-lined basket and serve immediately.

party prep
This may be prepared up to 8 hours ahead through step 3 (but do not preheat the oven) and refrigerated. Remove from the refrigerator 30 minutes before baking.

½ cup Parmesan Dip (page 60), at room temperature

½ teaspoon finely chopped fresh thyme

¼ teaspoon finely chopped fresh oregano, or a pinch of dried oregano

1 large loaf French, Italian, or sourdough bread

¼ cup freshly grated Parmesan cheese

parmesan dip

This all-purpose spread is served with slices of crusty bread at Bottega, the popular restaurant in California's Napa Valley. It is a pleasing alternative to butter or olive oil as an accompaniment for bread. And it comes together in just minutes in the food processor. Serve it in a ramekin with a small spoon. This is the base for the artichoke dip on the facing page and for making the delicious garlic bread on page 59. So you may want to double the recipe and freeze one batch to use later.

serves 8 to 12 (makes about 1 generous cup)

1 Mince the garlic in a food processor. Add the remaining ingredients and pulse for about 10 seconds to break the cheese into small granules. (Use a rubber spatula to scrape down the sides and recombine the mixture every couple of pulses.)

2 Transfer the dip to a sealed container and refrigerate for up to 2 weeks. Bring to room temperature before serving.

2 garlic cloves

¼ pound Parmesan cheese, broken into 1-inch chunks

¼ pound Pecorino Romano or Pecorino Toscano cheese, broken into 1-inch chunks

½ teaspoon freshly ground black pepper

1 tablespoon chopped fresh basil

2 tablespoons chopped fresh chives

½ teaspoon red pepper flakes

¾ cup olive oil

THE CLEVER COOK COULD:

- Use just one of the cheeses to simplify.

- Double the recipe for a large party.

- Serve the dip on toasted slices of French baguette.

parmesan-
artichoke dip

You'll find this recipe tastes lighter and fresher than other artichoke dips, which usually include mayonnaise and cream cheese. This is great for casual gatherings with a bowl of pita chips or bite-size pieces of baguette.

serves 8 to 12

¼ cup Parmesan Dip (facing page)

One 12-ounce jar marinated artichoke hearts, drained and coarsely chopped

1 teaspoon grated lemon zest

Red pepper flakes

1 Combine all the ingredients in a medium mixing bowl and blend well.

2 Transfer the dip to a sealed container and refrigerate for up to 2 days. Remove from the refrigerator 30 minutes before serving.

PUFF PASTRY APPETIZER BITES

The quality of store-bought puff pastry has drastically improved over the last few years, and it makes a great starting point for numerous party appetizers. You can adapt the following technique to practically any topping that will complement your menu. These little bites are simple, yet elegant.

MAKES ABOUT 12 BITES

One 10-x-9-x-⅛ inch frozen puff pastry dough sheet, defrosted

1 egg beaten with 2 tablespoons water

½ cup filling of your choice

1 Preheat the oven to 400°F. Line a baking sheet with parchment paper. Unfold the puff pastry sheet on a lightly floured surface. With a 2½- or 3-inch round floured cookie cutter, cut out the desired number of puff pastry bites, working quickly so the dough does not become too sticky to handle.

2 With a knife, lightly mark a border about ⅛ inch from the edge of each circle, being careful not to cut through the dough. Also make three slits in the middle of each circle without cutting through the bottom. Transfer to the baking sheet.

3 With a clean finger, moisten the border of each circle evenly with the egg wash so they will brown in the oven. Fill the center of each circle with a teaspoon or so of the desired filling.

4 Bake at 400°F for about 10 minutes, or until the pastry is golden brown. Serve warm or at room temperature.

Here are some filling ideas:

- Caramelized Onions (page 215) and Manchego cheese
- Sun-Dried Tomato Pesto (page 209) and freshly grated Parmesan cheese
- Shredded prosciutto and Gorgonzola cheese
- Chopped Brie cheese and green apple
- Chutney and grated sharp cheddar cheese

hawaiian ahi dip

This fish dip requires sushi-grade ahi tuna. I first tasted a version of this at the Kahala Hotel and Resort in Hawaii, and I have been making this adaptation ever since. Look for a good-quality pickled ginger (you can usually find it in the Asian section of the market). Some markets sell it next to the fresh sushi counter. It should taste slightly sweet and spicy.

I like to serve this on a platter with a combination of raw vegetables and crispy flatbread. To drink? Try a Hawaiian cocktail like a mai tai or perhaps a chilled Viognier or Pinot Gris wine. I suggest you enjoy this outside on a warm summer night. Not exactly Hawaii, but close enough.

serves 4 to 6

1 To make the dip: Chop the ahi tuna into ¼-inch pieces and set aside. Put the mayonnaise, sour cream, soy sauce, lemon juice, pickled ginger, sesame seeds, cilantro, and ¼ cup scallions in a medium bowl, and mix to combine. Season with salt and pepper. Add the chopped tuna and mix to combine.

2 Transfer the dip to a medium serving bowl and garnish with the 1 ounce of tuna and 1 tablespoon scallions. Serve with raw vegetables and/or sesame crackers.

party prep
This may be prepared up to 4 hours ahead, covered, and refrigerated.

dip

¼ pound sushi-grade ahi tuna, plus 1 ounce for garnish

½ cup mayonnaise

½ cup sour cream

1 teaspoon soy sauce

1 tablespoon fresh lemon juice

2 tablespoons finely chopped pickled ginger

1 teaspoon roasted sesame seeds

1 teaspoon finely chopped fresh cilantro

¼ cup thinly sliced scallions, green part only, or chives, plus 1 tablespoon for garnish

Salt and freshly ground black pepper

Raw vegetables or sesame crackers, or both, for serving

grilled artichoke halves
with grilled tomato aioli

People always seem surprised that artichokes can be grilled. Grilled artichokes, with their smoky flavor, taste decidedly different from steamed artichokes. I love to serve these at a casual dinner. If you prefer a lighter sauce, try the Buttermilk Garden Herb Dressing (page 205) instead of making the aioli.

serves 6

1 Cut the sharp points off the artichoke leaves with kitchen shears. Remove the small dry outer leaves from around the base of each artichoke. Cut off the stem 1 inch from the bottom. Soak the trimmed artichokes in cold water for at least 15 minutes to clean them.

2 Place the artichokes upright in a large pot. Add about 4 inches of water and the lemon slices. Cook, partially covered, over medium heat for 30 to 40 minutes, or until the leaves pull off fairly easily. (You want to make sure the artichokes will hold together when grilled.)

3 Remove the artichokes from the pot and cool to room temperature. Cut them in half lengthwise. Scoop out the fuzzy choke with a teaspoon and discard.

4 Preheat the grill to medium-high. Brush the leaf side of each artichoke half with some of the olive oil. Place on the grill, leaf-side down, and grill for 3 to 4 minutes, or until the artichokes have grill marks. Brush the cut side of the artichoke halves with olive oil and turn over. Grill until they have grill marks, about 3 to 4 minutes more.

5 Remove the artichoke halves to a platter. Dollop 2 tablespoons of the aioli in the center of each half. Sprinkle with the parsley just before serving. Provide small bowls for guests to discard the leaves.

3 large artichokes

3 slices lemon

¼ cup olive oil

¾ cup Grilled Tomato Aioli (page 210)

2 tablespoons finely chopped fresh parsley

party prep

The artichokes may be prepared through step 3 up to 1 day ahead, covered, and refrigerated. Bring to room temperature before grilling.

prosciutto-wrapped figs
with burrata & port & balsamic syrup

These are a hit at any party, and a snap to prepare. Make them when figs are in season, from summer to midfall. The Port & Balsamic Syrup elevates these fruit and cheese nuggets to a new level of deliciousness. It's fun to serve them on a platter so that guests can help themselves. You can offer little plates and forks, or just let your guests pick them up. Make sure to have cocktail napkins close by since these are a bit messy, but oh so worth it.

serves 8 to 12

3 ounces mozzarella or Burrata cheese

8 fresh figs, stems removed, halved (if large they can be quartered)

Freshly ground black pepper

16 thin slices prosciutto (about ½ pound)

Port & Balsamic Syrup (page 207)

1 Cut the cheese into ½-inch squares and press firmly into the center of the fig halves. Sprinkle the halves with black pepper.

2 Wrap 1 prosciutto slice around each fig half and place all of the figs on a platter.

3 Drizzle the syrup over the figs. Serve immediately.

party prep
This may be prepared through step 2 up to 6 hours in advance. Cover and refrigerate. Do step 3 just before serving.

tapas platter

This no-cook companion to Sangria (page 52) is best put together just before serving. Find a pretty wooden platter for presentation. Arrange toothpicks in a small dish or shot glass, and accompany the olives with a small bowl for discarded pits.

serves 8 to 12

1 Arrange the cheeses on a wooden platter. Place a ramekin of fig jam or tiny cubes of quince paste on the platter.

2 Arrange the meats on part of the platter so they are overlapping one another in an attractive design. Place the almonds in a small dish on the platter. Place the olives in a dish. Arrange the bread sticks on the platter so they overlap the meats, and serve.

party prep
The platter may be prepared up to 1 hour ahead, loosely covered with plastic, and kept at room temperature.

½ pound Manchego cheese, cut into 2 wedges

½ pound fresh goat cheese in a log

½ cup fig jam or quince paste, cut into ½-inch cubes

¼ pound salami, thinly sliced

¼ pound prosciutto, Serrano ham, or speck, thinly sliced

¼ pound mortadella, thinly sliced

1 cup Marcona almonds

2 cups mixed marinated olives

Bread sticks

mini-corn
& crab cakes
with grilled tomato aioli

Crab lovers flock to these little nuggets of Dungeness crab and corn kernels. Whenever I serve these at a party, I can always count on them to be the first appetizer to go. It's essential to use only the best crabmeat since that is the dominant flavor. Ask your fishmonger if you can taste the crab to make sure it's fresh and slightly sweet. Panko flakes, which are Japanese-style bread crumbs, are used here for a crispy coating.

serves 8 to 12

1 large egg, lightly beaten

2 tablespoons mayonnaise

1 teaspoon Dijon mustard

1 tablespoon finely chopped fresh chives

1 pound cooked Dungeness crabmeat, pulled apart into ½-inch chunks

½ cup fresh corn kernels (about 1 ear of corn)

½ cup fresh bread crumbs

Salt

Pinch of cayenne pepper

½ cup panko (Japanese-style bread crumbs)

2 tablespoons unsalted butter

2 tablespoons olive oil

½ cup Grilled Tomato Aioli (page 210)

1 In a large bowl, combine the egg, mayonnaise, mustard, and chives. Add the crabmeat, corn, and bread crumbs and mix well. Season with salt and the cayenne pepper.

2 Spread out the panko on a baking sheet. Divide the crab mixture into 18 equal portions. Shape each portion into a cake about 2 inches in diameter and ¾ inch thick and place on wax paper. Coat the crab cakes completely with the panko, and use a spatula to transfer them to a clean baking sheet. Cover with plastic wrap and refrigerate for at least 1 hour, or up to 6 hours.

3 Melt 1 tablespoon of the butter with 1 tablespoon of the olive oil in a large skillet over medium-high heat. Add half of the crab cakes and sauté, turning once with a spatula, until golden brown on both sides, about 2½ minutes per side. Repeat with the remaining butter, oil, and crab cakes.

4 Transfer the crab cakes to a platter and top each with a dollop of the aioli. Serve immediately.

party prep
The crab cakes may be prepared up to 6 hours ahead through step 2, covered, and refrigerated. These also can be sautéed and kept warm in a 300°F oven for about 30 minutes.

roasted
shrimp cocktail
with mango cocktail sauce

Roasting the shrimp in this updated classic makes all the difference. For a cocktail party, arrange the shrimp on a white platter with their tails all facing out in the same direction. For a first course, serve the shrimp in individual glass bowls or martini glasses. Accompany them with flatbread-style crackers.

serves 6 to 8 as a first course and 12 to 20 as an appetizer; mango cocktail sauce makes about 1 cup

1 Preheat the oven to 400°F. Put the shrimp on a large rimmed baking sheet. In a small bowl, combine the shallot, lemon zest and juice, olive oil, and seasoning salt and stir to blend. Pour over the shrimp and move them around to coat evenly. Make sure the shrimp are arranged in one layer, without overlapping.

2 Roast the shrimp for 8 to 9 minutes, or until they are pink and opaque all the way through. Transfer to a dish and let cool. Refrigerate until serving.

3 To prepare the cocktail sauce: In a food processor, purée the mango. Add the remaining ingredients and process until blended. Taste for seasoning.

4 **To serve as an appetizer—**Transfer the cocktail sauce to a small bowl and place in the center of a 12-inch round or rectangular platter. Arrange the shrimp around the outside of the platter in a pretty pattern. Garnish with the parsley. Make sure to have a small bowl next to the platter to dispose of the tails.

To serve as a first course—For each guest, spoon a couple of tablespoons of the cocktail sauce into a martini glass. Sprinkle the parsley on top of the sauce. Arrange 4 to 5 shrimp around the edge of the glass. Serve immediately.

party prep

The shrimp and sauce may be made up to 1 day ahead, covered, and refrigerated.

2 pounds large shrimp, peeled and deveined, with the tails kept on

1 shallot, finely chopped

Zest of 1 lemon

1 tablespoon fresh lemon juice

1 tablespoon olive oil

Seriously Simple Seasoning Salt (page 217) or store-bought seasoning salt

mango cocktail sauce

1 cup peeled and diced mango (about 1 medium ripe mango)

½ cup chili sauce

2 teaspoons cream-style horseradish

2 teaspoons fresh lime juice

A few drops of Worcestershire sauce

A few drops of hot sauce, or to taste

2 tablespoons finely chopped fresh parsley for garnish

THE CLEVER COOK COULD:

• Add a diced avocado to the sauce.

• Chop the shrimp coarsely, put in a large bowl, and add diced avocado. Stir in the sauce and serve in martini or cocktail glasses.

smoked salmon
with crispy shallots
& dilled cream

Easy to put together, this has a big wow factor. The smoked salmon, crispy sweet shallots, and dilled cream sauce come together for a dish that is more than the sum of its parts. These bites are great for a romantic dinner party, but they are also an elegant addition to a cocktail party.

serves 4 to 6

1 To make the sauce: Combine the sour cream, dill, and lemon juice in a small bowl and stir to blend well. Season with salt and pepper and set aside.

2 Heat the olive oil and butter in a large skillet over medium-high heat. Add the shallots and sauté for 3 to 5 minutes, or until crisp and golden brown, stirring the shallots to make sure they don't burn. Drain on paper towels and then transfer to a small bowl and set aside.

3 Arrange the bread or crackers on a platter. Place a small spoonful of dilled sauce on each. Arrange a salmon slice, rolled up to look like a rose, on top of each bread slice or cracker. Top with a dollop of the dilled sauce and sprinkle with the crispy shallots. Serve immediately.

party prep
This may be prepared through step 2 up to 2 hours ahead. Refrigerate the sauce and leave the shallots at room temperature.

sauce
½ cup sour cream or crème fraîche

1 tablespoon finely chopped fresh dill weed

1½ teaspoons fresh lemon juice

Salt and freshly ground white pepper

¼ cup olive oil

2 tablespoons unsalted butter

8 medium shallots, thinly sliced

12 French baguette slices or Carr's water biscuits

6 slices good-quality smoked salmon, each halved lengthwise

grilled chicken skewers
with yogurt-mango curry sauce

These chicken skewers with Indian flavors are always a hit at cocktail parties. Be sure to soak the bamboo skewers in water for at least 30 minutes, or even overnight, to prevent flare-ups when grilling. This recipe can be doubled, tripled, or made for as many people as you like. A chilled Riesling or Gewürztraminer would be a refreshing accompaniment. Or serve cold Indian beer.

serves 8

1   To make the marinade: In a medium nonreactive bowl, combine the yogurt, olive oil, lime zest and juice, red pepper flakes, and pepper.

2   Add the chicken to the marinade and toss to coat well. Cover and refrigerate for at least 2 hours, but no longer than 4 hours.

3   To make the sauce: Combine yogurt, curry powder, lime zest and juice, and chutney in a medium bowl. Stir to combine and season with red pepper flakes, salt, and pepper. Cover and refrigerate until serving.

4   Thread two pieces of chicken, one at a time, on a bamboo skewer, covering only the top third of each skewer.

5   Preheat an outdoor grill to medium-high, or heat a lightly oiled grill pan over medium-high heat. Grill the skewers for approximately 3 minutes per side, or until the chicken is cooked through, with no trace of pink remaining.

6   To serve, arrange the skewers on a platter in a circular design, with the chicken facing in. Spoon the sauce into a small serving bowl and place in the center of the platter.

party prep

The chicken may be prepared through step 4 up to 4 hours ahead, covered, and refrigerated. The sauce may be made 1 day ahead, covered, and refrigerated.

marinade

½ cup plain low-fat Greek yogurt

2 tablespoons olive oil

Zest of ½ lime

1 teaspoon fresh lime juice

Pinch of red pepper flakes

Freshly ground black pepper

1½ lbs chicken tenders, halved lengthwise

sauce

1¼ cups plain low-fat Greek yogurt

1¾ teaspoons curry powder

Zest of 1 lime

1 teaspoon fresh lime juice

½ cup mango chutney, mashed with a fork to break up large pieces

Red pepper flakes

Salt and freshly ground black pepper

chicken drumettes
with romesco sauce

This grown-up version of a kid-friendly dish is a crowd-pleaser for all ages. These baby chicken drumsticks (really part of the wing) are bathed in a red pepper and lemon marinade. Romesco Sauce (page 213), a blend of roasted red peppers, sweet Marcona almonds, and paprika, is the big flavor here. It is used in the marinade and also as a dipping sauce for the golden brown drumettes, so be sure to make it before you begin this dish. (You'll need 1 whole recipe of the romesco.) Serve this during football season as a tasty bite before the main meal.

serves 8

1   To make the marinade: In the food processor, mince the garlic and then add the roasted pepper and purée them. Add the lemon juice, olive oil, romesco sauce, red pepper flakes, and sugar; season with salt; and purée until combined.

2   Combine the marinade with the drumettes in a large lock-top plastic bag. Press out the air and seal. Move the chicken around so it is evenly coated and marinate for at least 2 hours and up to 8 hours.

3   Preheat the oven to 425°F. Arrange the drumettes on a baking sheet in one layer. Roast for 25 minutes, or until nicely browned, and then turn them with tongs. Roast for 30 minutes more, or until nicely browned.

4   Place the drumettes on a serving platter and accompany with romesco sauce on the side. Serve immediately.

party prep

These may be made through step 3 up to 2 days in advance. Cool the drumettes, cover, and refrigerate. Before the party, bring the chicken to room temperature and place on a baking sheet. Preheat the oven to 425°F. Reheat the chicken for about 15 minutes, or until heated through, and serve.

marinade

3 garlic cloves, minced

1 roasted red pepper

¼ cup fresh lemon juice

⅓ cup olive oil

½ cup Romesco Sauce (page 213), plus 1 cup for serving

½ teaspoon red pepper flakes

Pinch of sugar, if too tart

Salt

24 chicken drumettes (about 4½ pounds)

THE CLEVER COOK COULD:

• Double or triple this recipe for a big crowd.

• Use the marinade on chicken parts and roast.

soups & salads

white gazpacho

Guests will be happily surprised with this take on gazpacho. Creamy white in color, it is a cool and refreshing soup for a hot summer day. Serve it with the Tapas Platter (page 66) and a variety of breads for a small lunchtime gathering, or as a prelude to dinner. It is the perfect beginning for Oven-Baked Paella (page 121) or Grilled Chicken with Green Bean, Sweet Pepper & Tomato Salad & Romesco Sauce (page 130).

serves 6

1 In a food processor, mince the garlic. Cut a cucumber half into chunks and add to the food processor, along with the 1 cup of the grapes. Process for about 20 seconds, or until puréed. Add the bread and purée again.

2 Combine the yogurt and broth in a medium bowl. Add the puréed cucumber mixture, olive oil, vinegar, parsley, chives, and ½ cup of the almonds. Mix until well combined.

3 Chop the remaining cucumber half into small dice and add to the soup mixture. Add the cayenne and season with salt and pepper. Refrigerate until chilled, at least 4 hours.

4 Cut the remaining ¼ cup of grapes in half and transfer to a small bowl. Add the remaining 2 tablespoons chopped almonds and toss with the grapes.

5 To serve, pour the gazpacho into individual soup bowls and garnish with the grape and almond mixture.

party prep

The soup may be prepared up to 8 hours ahead, covered, and refrigerated. Taste for seasoning before serving.

2 medium garlic cloves

1 European cucumber, halved lengthwise and seeded

1¼ cups green grapes

2 slices white bread, crusts removed, and cut into 2-inch pieces

1½ cups low-fat Greek yogurt

1½ cups chicken or vegetable broth

¼ cup olive oil

2 tablespoons sherry vinegar

2 tablespoons chopped fresh parsley

2 tablespoons finely chopped fresh chives

½ cup plus 2 tablespoons roasted and salted Spanish Marcona almonds, coarsely chopped

Pinch of cayenne pepper

Salt and freshly ground white pepper

chilled buttermilk corn soup

Corn soups taste best in the summer, when corn is at its peak. You can use either white or yellow for this recipe. Corn quickly turns to starch and the flavors fade, so find the freshest corn possible, and sample some to make sure the corn is sweet and crisp. Husk the corn and remove the kernels. The easiest way to do this is to place the corn vertically in a shallow bowl and slide a very sharp knife down the corn, releasing the kernels into the bowl. Turn the corn and continue.

serves 6

2 tablespoons olive oil

2 medium leeks, cleaned, white and light green parts only, finely chopped

6 cups fresh corn kernels (about 6 to 7 large or 12 medium ears)

2 garlic cloves, minced

6 cups chicken or vegetable broth

1 cup buttermilk, plus extra for drizzling on the soup

Salt and freshly ground white pepper

3 tablespoons finely chopped fresh chives for garnish

1 In a large saucepan, heat the olive oil over medium heat. Add the leeks and sauté for 7 to 10 minutes, stirring frequently, until nicely softened and lightly browned. Add all but ½ cup of the corn kernels and continue to cook for about another 2 minutes. Add the garlic and cook for another 1 minute.

2 Add the broth, raise the heat to high, and bring to a boil. Reduce the heat and simmer, partially covered, for about 10 minutes, or until the corn is soft.

3 Purée the soup in the pan with an immersion blender or cool slightly and purée in a blender. Pass through a food mill or a fine-mesh strainer, pressing on the pulp to get all of the flavor. Chill for at least 4 hours. Add the 1 cup buttermilk and season with salt and pepper.

4 Immerse the remaining ½ cup corn kernels in boiling water for about 1 minute. Drain and cool.

5 To serve, pour the soup into bowls or mugs and garnish with a drizzle of buttermilk, the cooked corn kernels, and the chives.

party prep
The soup may be made ahead, covered, and refrigerated for up to 2 days. Taste and readjust the seasonings before serving.

soups & salads

cucumber, pea & mint soup

The cucumber, mint, and peas seem made for each other in this cup of green, cooling comfort. To make it Seriously Simple, make the soup with frozen petite peas that have been defrosted. Just make sure it is very cold. This is one of those soups that makes a great starter for many dishes, like the Italian Picnic Sandwich (page 109), Deli Frittata (page 107), or Pomegranate-Marinated Grilled Lamb Chops (page 149).

serves 4 to 6

1 To make the soup: Cut three-quarters of the cucumber into 2-inch chunks. (Dice the rest finely and set aside for the relish.)

2 In a large blender, combine the cucumber chunks, peas, scallions, mint, and broth and blend on high until completely puréed. Add the sour cream and lemon juice, season with salt and pepper, and blend well. Taste for seasoning. (If the soup is not totally smooth you can pour it through a fine-mesh strainer over a bowl.) Refrigerate the soup until chilled, at least 4 hours.

3 To make the relish: Combine the diced cucumber, peas, mint, and lemon juice in a small bowl. Season with salt and pepper and mix to blend well. Taste for seasoning.

4 Just before serving, stir the soup, which may have separated during refrigeration. Pour the soup into small bowls and garnish with the sour cream and relish. Serve immediately.

party prep

This may be made through step 3 up to a day ahead, covered, and refrigerated. Readjust the seasonings and mix to blend well before serving.

soup

1 European cucumber

2 cups fresh shelled peas (about 2 pounds unshelled), or 2 cups frozen petits pois (small peas), defrosted

4 scallions, light green and white parts only, thinly sliced

3 tablespoons chopped fresh mint

4 cups chicken or vegetable broth

¼ cup sour cream

1 tablespoon fresh lemon juice

Salt and freshly ground white pepper

relish

¼ European cucumber, finely diced (reserved from making the soup)

⅓ cup frozen petits pois (small peas), defrosted

2 tablespoons finely chopped fresh mint

1 teaspoon fresh lemon juice

Salt and freshly ground black pepper

¼ cup sour cream for garnish

smoky tomato soup

Canned fire-roasted tomatoes add a delicious smoky flavor to this soup, and also a welcoming wave of heat, which is enhanced by a dash of chipotle Tabasco sauce. Serve this as a starter or as part of a main course, along with your favorite grilled cheese sandwich. The Herbed Garlic Cheese Bread (page 59) would make a tasty accompaniment.

serves 6 to 8

1 In a medium soup pot, heat the olive oil over medium-high heat. Add the leeks and sauté for 4 to 5 minutes, or until softened. Add the carrots and celery and cook for another 4 minutes, or until they begin to soften. Add the garlic and cook for 1 minute, or until slightly softened.

2 Sprinkle the flour over the vegetables, reduce the heat to low, and continue to cook, stirring constantly, for 1 minute, or until the flour is thickened and incorporated into the vegetables. Add the tomatoes, tomato paste, sugar, and broth; raise the heat to medium-high; and bring to a simmer.

3 Partially cover the pan, reduce the heat to medium, and cook, stirring occasionally, for 15 minutes, or until the vegetables are tender and all the flavors are well blended. With an immersion blender, purée the soup, or if you prefer a finer texture, use a blender. (If using a blender, cool the soup and hold the top down so that there won't be any unwanted surprises.) If you want your soup totally smooth, pour it through a fine-mesh sieve after you have blended it.

4 Add the milk to the soup over medium heat, stirring to combine, and cook for another minute. Add the chipotle sauce and season with salt. (If you prefer the soup thinner, add more milk or broth to reach the desired consistency.)

5 Ladle the soup into soup bowls and garnish each bowl with a few croutons before serving.

party prep

The soup may be prepared ahead through step 3, covered, and refrigerated for up to 2 days or frozen for up to 1 month. Defrost and warm the soup, and proceed with the recipe.

¼ cup olive oil

4 leeks, light green and white parts only, cleaned and finely chopped

2 medium carrots, peeled and finely chopped

2 ribs celery, finely chopped

3 garlic cloves, minced

2 tablespoons all-purpose flour

Three 14½-ounce cans fire-roasted diced tomatoes, with their juice

6 tablespoons tomato paste

1½ teaspoons sugar, or to taste

5 cups chicken or vegetable broth

1¼ cups milk or half-and-half

½ teaspoon Tabasco chipotle sauce, or to taste

Salt

¾ cup croutons, preferably cheese or garlic, for garnish

THE CLEVER COOK COULD:

- Serve this in little cups to welcome your guests on a chilly night.

- Add a rind of Parmesan cheese to the soup while it is cooking. Remove the rind before adding the milk, and garnish each serving with freshly grated Parmesan cheese.

- Serve this with Parmesan Bagel Crisps (page 216).

turkey vegetable soup with pesto

Parties don't always have to have lots of courses. Sometimes I want a casual gathering with just a great pot of soup and maybe a salad and a basket of bread. Many of these get-togethers are more memorable than the more formal dinner parties I have hosted. Try this when it's really cold out and you don't feel like making a major menu. Orzo pasta, turkey, and an assertive pesto balance one another in a most pleasing way. Serve this with Herbed Garlic Cheese Bread (page 59) or warm sourdough bread for a satisfying lunch or dinner.

serves 8 as a main course

1 Put the turkey thigh in a large saucepan and add 8 cups of water. Bring to a boil over medium-high heat, reduce the heat, and simmer for about 45 minutes, or until the thigh is partially cooked. Remove from the heat and let the turkey cool in the broth.

2 Heat the olive oil in a 6-quart soup pot over medium heat. Add the onion and sauté for 3 to 5 minutes, or until the onion is softened, stirring occasionally. Add the carrots, zucchini, and eggplants and sauté for about 3 minutes, stirring frequently. Add the garlic and sauté for 1 minute longer.

3 Add the partially cooked turkey thigh, reserving the broth. Add the tomatoes and basil. Measure the turkey broth, add it to the pot, and add enough water to make 12 cups of liquid. Bring to a simmer, reduce the heat, and simmer until all the vegetables are tender, about 15 minutes. Remove 2 cups of the soup to a small pot and purée with an immersion blender. Return the purée to the remaining soup. Add the orzo, beans, and Swiss chard and cook for about 15 minutes, or until the orzo is cooked.

4 Remove the turkey thigh from the pot. Let cool and cut the meat from the bones. Shred the meat into bite-size pieces and return it to the pot. Season with salt and pepper and the $1/3$ cup pesto. Taste for seasoning.

5 Ladle the hot soup into soup bowls and swirl about a teaspoon of the remaining pesto into each bowl. Serve immediately.

1 turkey thigh (about ¾ pound), skinned

2 tablespoons olive oil

1 medium onion, finely chopped

4 carrots, peeled and cut into ½-inch pieces

4 zucchini, cut into 1-inch pieces

2 Japanese eggplants, unpeeled, cut into 1-inch pieces

2 garlic cloves, minced

One 14½-ounce can diced tomatoes, drained

2 tablespoons finely chopped fresh basil, or 1 tablespoon dried

⅓ cup orzo

2 cups cooked white beans, such as cannellini, or one 15-ounce can, drained and rinsed well

1 large bunch red Swiss chard, coarsely shredded

Salt and freshly ground black pepper

⅓ cup Sun-Dried Tomato Pesto (page 209) or your favorite pesto, plus 3 tablespoons

party prep

The soup and pesto may be prepared up to 3 days ahead and refrigerated. Bring both to room temperature, heat the soup, and serve. This soup also freezes well. Be sure to adjust the seasonings after you reheat the frozen soup.

cabbage &
apple slaw
with agave-citrus dressing

Coleslaw takes just a few minutes to put together now that fresh shredded coleslaw vegetables are readily available. The nonfat yogurt in the dressing lightens up this version, while agave syrup adds a touch of sweetness. Try this with grilled ribs on a summer night, or bring it along on a picnic. It also goes well with sandwiches, hamburgers, or barbecued chicken.

serves 8 to 10

1 To make the dressing: Combine the mayonnaise, yogurt, agave syrup, lemon juice, and vinegar in the bottom of a medium serving bowl. Season with salt and pepper and whisk well until blended.

2 Add the apple and coleslaw mix and toss with tongs until all of the cabbage and apple are coated.

3 Refrigerate for at least 1 hour to allow the flavors to meld. Garnish with the parsley before serving.

party prep
This can be made 1 day ahead, covered, and refrigerated. Toss before serving.

dressing
¾ cup mayonnaise

¾ cup nonfat Greek yogurt

1½ tablespoons agave syrup

1½ tablespoons fresh lemon juice

1 tablespoon cider vinegar

Salt and freshly ground black pepper

1 Fuji or Granny Smith apple, peeled and shredded

Two 1-pound packages shredded coleslaw mix

2 tablespoons finely chopped fresh parsley or dill weed for garnish

"the wedge"
with blue cheese dressing, pancetta & cherry tomatoes

Some dishes never go out of style. This is one of them. And it is so easy to make; you just brown the pancetta and cut up heads of iceberg lettuce. The crisp lettuce wedges are presented with a topping of blue cheese vinaigrette, crumbles of the pancetta and blue cheese, and sweet cherry tomatoes. For a dinner party, serve these on individual salad plates or arrange the wedges on a large platter and dress them just before serving.

serves 8

1 To make the dressing: Combine the vinegar, olive oil, and sour cream in a medium bowl and whisk to blend together. Use an immersion blender to emulsify the dressing. Add the Worcestershire sauce and blue cheese and mix well. With the back of a fork, mash some of the cheese crumbles into the dressing. Season with salt and pepper.

2 To make the salad: Brown the pancetta in a medium skillet over medium heat for 6 to 7 minutes, or until crisp. Remove with a slotted spoon and drain on paper towels. Let cool and reserve.

3 Remove the core of the lettuce by first hitting the lettuce against the counter to loosen the core. Cut each head into four equal wedges.

4 Arrange the wedges on a large platter. Spoon the dressing over the lettuce. Spoon over each wedge an equal amount of the pancetta, chopped tomatoes, and blue cheese. Serve immediately.

party prep
The salad may be prepared through step 2 up to 4 hours ahead. Refrigerate the dressing and leave the pancetta, covered, at room temperature. Before serving, bring the dressing to room temperature and whisk, as it may separate while sitting.

dressing
¼ cup red wine vinegar

½ cup olive oil

¼ cup sour cream

1 teaspoon Worcestershire sauce

⅓ cup crumbled blue cheese

Salt and freshly ground black pepper

salad
¼ pound pancetta, finely diced

2 medium heads iceberg lettuce

½ cup yellow and red cherry tomatoes, finely chopped

2 tablespoons crumbled blue cheese

seriously simple parties

SEASONAL FRUIT SALADS

Although there are more options for fruit salad in the summer months, by using seasonal fruits, you can make a delicious salad to complement a meal any time of the year. Here are a few suggestions for how to put together a fruit salad in any season.

SERVES 8

8 cups fresh fruit (see following suggestions)

2 tablespoons finely chopped fresh mint or 2 tablespoons liqueur

DIPPING SAUCE

1 cup plain nonfat Greek yogurt

2 tablespoons honey

1 teaspoon grated lemon zest

1 Toss the fruit together in a bowl. Add the fresh mint to brighten up the flavors, or to make a dressed-up version, try adding a complementary fruit liqueur.

2 To make the dipping sauce: Stir together the yogurt, honey, and lemon zest. Serve alongside the fruit salad.

SPRING

- Apricots, pitted and quartered and cut into 2-inch pieces
- Strawberries, hulled and sliced
- Pineapple, peeled and cut into 2-inch cubes
- Optional liqueur: Noyau de Poissy (apricot liqueur)

SUMMER

- Watermelon, cut into 2-inch cubes or scooped with a melon baller
- Cantaloupe or Tuscan melon, cut into 2-inch cubes or scooped with a melon baller
- Blackberries or raspberries
- Peaches, quartered and cut into 2-inch pieces
- Optional liqueur: limoncello

AUTUMN

- Green apples, cored and cut into 2-inch cubes
- Red grapes
- Fresh figs, quartered, or dried figs, cut into 2-inch cubes
- Optional liqueur: pear liqueur

WINTER

- Satsumas, peeled and sectioned
- Papayas, peeled and cut into 2-inch cubes. Add the seeds to the salad for a unique flavor and texture.
- Kiwis, peeled and quartered and cut into 2-inch cubes
- Optional liqueur: Orange liqueur like Grand Marnier or Cointreau

mixed greens
with edamame pesto crostini

This colorful salad includes edamame (green soybeans), which are added to the greens along with bright red and yellow cherry tomatoes and crumbles of creamy feta or goat cheese. The edamame are also the surprise ingredient in the pesto, which is spooned on top of the baguette toasts, or crostini. The toasts are arranged around the salad for a pretty garnish.

serves 8 to 12

1 Preheat the oven to 350°F. Put the bread on a baking sheet and coat the slices with cooking spray. Toast for 5 minutes on each side, or until they are lightly browned and crispy. Set aside while they cool.

2 To make the vinaigrette: Combine the shallot, garlic, parsley, mustard, and red wine vinegar in a medium bowl and whisk until well blended. (Or combine in a food processor and process until well blended.) Slowly pour the olive oil into the bowl, whisking continuously (or processing) until blended. Season with salt and pepper.

3 In a large salad bowl, combine the greens, tomatoes, edamame, and cheese. Drizzle on enough vinaigrette to lightly moisten the salad.

4 Spread a tablespoon of pesto on each toast and arrange around the outer rim of the salad bowl in a circular design. Serve immediately, with the remaining dressing on the side.

party prep
The dressing may be made 3 days ahead, covered, and kept at room temperature. The toasts may be prepared up to 4 hours ahead, cooled, and kept at room temperature.

Twelve ½-inch-thick baguette slices, cut on a bias

Olive oil cooking spray

vinaigrette

1 medium shallot, finely chopped

1 garlic clove, minced

2 tablespoons finely chopped fresh parsley

2 teaspoons whole-grain mustard

¼ cup red wine vinegar

¾ cup olive oil

Salt and freshly ground black pepper

1 pound mixed spring greens

One 12-ounce container yellow and red cherry tomatoes

1½ cups frozen shelled edamame, defrosted

1 cup crumbled feta or fresh goat cheese

Edamame Pesto (page 208)

THE CLEVER COOK COULD:

• Serve the pesto crostini as appetizers.

arugula salad
with roasted grapes

This unusual salad is good as a starter or after the main course. Make up the dressing ahead of time, since you will need to roast the shallots and garlic first. The roasted large seedless grapes shrink when they cook and become sweet and sour, offering a burst of fruity flavor to the bitter greens, creamy cheese, and crisp almonds. Marcona almonds are sold blanched and lightly fried or roasted and have a decidedly sweeter and more delicate texture than other almonds.

serves 6 to 8

1 To make the vinaigrette: Preheat the oven to 375°F. Place the shallots and garlic on a baking sheet. Coat them with the olive oil and season with salt and pepper. Roast them for about 45 minutes, or until browned and lightly caramelized, turning them midway through roasting. Let cool.

2 In a small food processor, combine the shallots and garlic and purée. Add the vinegar, mustard, and olive oil and blend until the dressing is emulsified. Season with salt and pepper. Before serving, stir the dressing thoroughly.

3 To make the salad: Increase the oven temperature to 450°F. Put the grapes on a baking sheet, drizzle with the olive oil, and sprinkle with salt. Roll around the grapes until evenly coated. Roast for about 15 minutes, or until lightly browned. Let cool.

4 Combine the arugula, grapes, cheese, and almonds in a large salad bowl. Pour enough dressing over the salad to moisten it, and mix to combine. Divide among salad plates and serve.

party prep
The vinaigrette may be prepared up to 1 week ahead, covered, and refrigerated. Bring to room temperature and whisk before using. The grapes can be roasted 8 hours ahead, covered, and refrigerated. The salad can be prepared up to 2 hours ahead, covered, and refrigerated. Dress the salad just before serving.

roasted shallot & garlic vinaigrette
6 medium shallots

4 garlic cloves, ends removed

1 tablespoon olive oil

Salt and freshly ground black pepper

¼ cup sherry vinegar

1 teaspoon Dijon Mustard

¾ cup olive oil

salad
50 Thompson seedless grapes

1 tablespoon olive oil

Salt

¾ pound arugula

½ cup shaved Manchego cheese

½ cup Marcona almonds

THE CLEVER COOK COULD:

- Try other seedless grape varieties. They should be large because they shrink as they cook.

- Use the dressing on many other salad greens or as a marinade for chicken or fish.

- Double the vinaigrette for a larger salad.

- Use toasted pine nuts, walnuts, or pecans instead of the Marcona almonds.

summer caprese salad with watermelon, cucumber & feta relish

Here is an updated variation on the layered mozzarella and tomato salad known as caprese. Like the classic version, it's simple to put together. Large ripe, red tomatoes are sliced and arranged on a platter, and a spoonful of the refreshing watermelon, cucumber, and feta relish is placed on top of each slice. Make sure to have a couple of serving spoons, so your guests can transfer both the tomatoes and the relish to their plates.

serves 6 to 8

1 To make the relish: Combine the watermelon, cucumber, feta, basil and mint in a medium bowl (being careful not to break the watermelon into smaller pieces) and set aside.

2 To make the dressing: Pour the red wine vinegar into a small bowl. While whisking, slowly pour in the olive oil in a steady stream and continue whisking until the dressing is emulsified. Add the chives and season with salt and pepper.

3 Just before serving, arrange the mixed greens in the center of a large round platter. Slice the tomatoes 1½ inches thick and arrange on a platter in a circular pattern, overlapping the slices.

4 Pour about half of the dressing over the relish and mix to combine. Taste for seasoning. Place a spoonful of relish on each tomato slice. Drizzle with the remaining dressing and serve immediately.

party prep
The relish and dressing may be made up to 2 hours ahead, covered, and kept at room temperature. It is best to slice the tomatoes and finish the salad just before serving.

relish
1½ cups diced seedless yellow or red watermelon (½-inch dice)

1½ cups diced European cucumber (½-inch dice)

¾ cup crumbled feta cheese

2 tablespoons finely chopped fresh basil

1 tablespoon finely chopped fresh mint

dressing
¼ cup red wine vinegar

½ cup extra-virgin olive oil

2 tablespoons finely chopped fresh chives

Salt and freshly ground black pepper

2 cups mixed greens, such as spring greens or mâche

6 large ripe beefsteak tomatoes

THE CLEVER COOK COULD:

- Substitute diced or tiny balls of fresh mozzarella or crumbled fresh goat cheese for the feta.

- Double the recipe.

- Make individual towers for a more formal presentation. For each serving, place a slice of tomato on a salad plate and add a spoonful of relish. Top with another tomato and more relish.

baby spinach salad
with winter squash & bacon

Smoky bacon pieces and sweet roasted squash make a tasty counterpoint to the spinach in this attractive salad. You can find prepared peeled and diced butternut squash in many supermarkets, which is a big time-saver. The salad is lightly dressed with a simple honey mustard and sherry vinaigrette.

serves 6

1 To make the dressing: In a small bowl, whisk the vinegar, lemon juice, mustard, and olive oil together. Season with salt and pepper and reserve.

2 To make the salad: In a medium skillet, cook the bacon over medium heat for 8 to 10 minutes, turning once, or until brown and crisp. Drain on paper towels. Cool and crumble the bacon into small pieces and set aside.

3 Preheat the oven to 425°F. Put the squash on a rimmed baking sheet. Drizzle with the olive oil and maple syrup, sprinkle with the seasoning salt, and toss to evenly coat the squash. Roast for 30 to 40 minutes, or until lightly browned, turning the squash once. Let cool and reserve.

4 Combine the spinach, squash, and bacon in a salad bowl. Drizzle the vinaigrette over all and toss to mix well. Serve immediately.

party prep
The salad can be prepared through step 3 up to 6 hours ahead and kept at room temperature. Cover the squash loosely.

dressing
3 tablespoons sherry vinegar

1 tablespoon fresh lemon juice

1 teaspoon honey Dijon mustard

½ cup olive oil

Salt and freshly ground black pepper

salad
½ pound applewood-smoked sliced bacon

2 pounds peeled, seeded, and cubed butternut squash

2 tablespoons olive oil

1 tablespoon maple syrup

Seriously Simple Seasoning Salt (page 217) or store-bought seasoning salt

¾ pound baby spinach leaves

green bean, sweet pepper & tomato salad

A simple citrus dressing highlights this lively vegetable mélange, without overpowering the distinctive flavor of each vegetable. Make sure to select small, sweet green beans for optimum texture and flavor. All you need for this salad is a saucepan and a serving bowl, so there is little cleanup. I like to serve this with chilled salmon or chicken. It's also a good addition to a group of salads for a simple luncheon.

serves 6

1 To make the dressing: In a medium serving bowl, combine the olive oil and lemon juice. Season with salt and pepper and whisk to blend.

2 To make the salad: Bring a medium saucepan of water to a boil. Add the green beans and cook for 7 to 10 minutes, depending on their size. The beans should still be slightly crisp. Drain well and rinse with cold water to stop the cooking. When cooled, add the beans to the bowl with the dressing. Add the bell pepper, tomatoes, and basil to the green beans. Toss with the dressing to combine. Taste for seasoning, and refrigerate until ready to serve.

party prep
The salad may be made up to 8 hours ahead, covered, and refrigerated.

dressing
¼ cup plus 1 tablespoon olive oil

2 tablespoons fresh lemon juice

Salt and freshly ground black pepper

salad
2 pounds small, tender green beans, ends trimmed

1 medium yellow bell pepper, seeded and julienned

1 cup cherry or grape red tomatoes

¼ cup torn fresh basil leaves

THE CLEVER COOK COULD:

- Make this into a main course salad by adding cooked shrimp, turkey, or chicken.

quinoa salad
with pomegranates & persimmons

The brilliant autumnal colors of orange persimmon and ruby-red pomegranate make this a perfect salad for the buffet table. Make sure to select a fuyu persimmon (it resembles a squat tomato) as it is slightly sweet and crisp. It's best to add the dressing just before serving so that the flavors stay fresh. Quinoa, a healthful grain, is easy to cook and has a very pleasing texture. I like to serve this with cold roast chicken or turkey.

serves 8 to 10

1   To make the dressing: In a medium bowl, whisk together the lemon juice, pomegranate juice, and mustard. Add the olive oil, whisking until incorporated. Season with salt and pepper and set aside.

2   To make the salad: Pour the quinoa into a bowl of cold water and wash it, rubbing it between your hands. Drain and repeat until the water is clear. Bring the 4 cups water and quinoa to a boil in a large saucepan. Stir once and cook, uncovered, over medium-high heat for about 10 minutes, or until the liquid is absorbed. Transfer to a large bowl. Let cool.

3   Add the persimmons and pomegranate seeds to the quinoa. Mix with a fork to keep the quinoa fluffy. Add the parsley and chives.

4   Pour the dressing over the grains and fruit and mix with the fork. Carefully add the feta cheese. Taste for seasoning and chill for at least 2 hours. Serve.

party prep

The salad may be prepared through step 3 up to 8 hours ahead, covered, and refrigerated. Remove 15 minutes before serving. Just before serving add the dressing and cheese and mix together. Taste and adjust the seasoning.

dressing

¼ cup fresh lemon juice

3 tablespoons pomegranate juice

1 tablespoon whole-grain mustard

½ cup olive oil

Salt and freshly ground black pepper

salad

2 cups quinoa

4 cups water or chicken or vegetable broth

3 fuyu persimmons, peeled and finely diced

1 cup pomegranate seeds

¼ cup finely chopped fresh parsley

2 tablespoons finely chopped fresh chives

1¼ cups crumbled feta or fresh goat cheese

THE CLEVER COOK COULD:

- Make this a year-round salad. Substitute white wine vinegar for the pomegranate juice. Omit the persimmmons and pomegranate seeds, and add to the quinoa ½ cup diced radishes, ½ cup diced European cucumber, 1 cup diced peeled carrrots, and 2 tablespoons finely chopped fresh mint.

orzo vegetable salad

Pasta salads have become old hat, but you'll find this one a colorful, textural delight. Crisp red radishes, moist green cucumber, and sweet orange carrots enliven the tiny, plain orzo. Fresh herbs and crumbled fresh goat cheese complete the salad. Try this for picnics, lunches, or on a summertime buffet table.

serves 8

1 To make the dressing: In a medium bowl, whisk together the garlic, mustard, red wine vinegar, balsamic vinegar, and olive oil until well combined. Season with salt and pepper.

2 Bring a large pot of salted water to a boil. Add the orzo and cook for 9 to 11 minutes, or until just done. Drain in a colander and transfer to a large mixing bowl. Add the olive oil to keep the pasta from sticking together. Let cool.

3 When the orzo is cool, add the cucumber, radishes, and carrots. Mix well. Add the chopped basil, chives, and parsley. Add the goat cheese, being careful not to mash it up.

4 Pour the dressing over the mixture and toss to mix the ingredients. Taste for seasoning. Transfer to a serving bowl and garnish with the basil leaves. Chill until serving.

party prep
The salad may be prepared 1 day ahead, covered, and refrigerated.

dressing
1 garlic clove, minced

2 teaspoons Dijon mustard

3 tablespoons red wine vinegar

1 tablespoon balsamic vinegar

½ cup olive oil

Salt and freshly ground black pepper

2 cups orzo

1 tablespoon olive oil

¾ cup finely diced European cucumber

8 radishes, finely diced

2 medium carrots, peeled and finely diced

5 ounces fresh goat cheese, crumbled

3 tablespoons finely chopped fresh basil, plus whole fresh basil leaves for garnish

2 tablespoons finely chopped fresh parsley

2 tablespoons finely chopped fresh chives

THE CLEVER COOK COULD:

• Substitute other cheeses like feta for the goat cheese, or omit the cheese altogether.

potato salad
with sun-dried tomato– caper vinaigrette

This zesty take on potato salad has no dairy in it, so you can serve it at an outside gathering without worrying about leaving it out in the sun. Much of the flavor comes from the sun-dried tomato pesto, balsamic vinegar, and capers. Take this on your next picnic or potluck.

serves 6 to 8

1 To make the vinaigrette: In a small bowl, combine both vinegars, the mustard, tomato pesto, capers, and parsley. Season with salt and pepper and whisk well to combine. Add the olive oil in a slow, steady stream, whisking constantly, until the vinaigrette is emulsified.

2 In a large pot of boiling water, cook the potatoes for 20 to 25 minutes, or until tender but slightly resistant when pierced with a fork. Drain and cool slightly. If large, cut into 1½-inch chunks and put in a medium mixing bowl.

3 Pour the vinaigrette over the potatoes and mix gently until coated. Taste for seasoning. Transfer to a serving bowl and refrigerate for at least 1 hour.

4 Remove the potato salad from the refrigerator 1 hour before serving. Garnish with the parsley and serve.

party prep
The potato salad may be prepared 1 day ahead, covered, and refrigerated. Make sure to remove from the refrigerator 1 hour before serving.

vinaigrette
¼ cup white balsamic vinegar

1 teaspoon balsamic vinegar

1 teaspoon Dijon mustard

2 tablespoons Sun-Dried Tomato Pesto (page 209) or store-bought

2 tablespoons drained and rinsed capers

2 tablespoons chopped fresh parsley

Salt and freshly ground black pepper

½ cup olive oil

3 pounds small potatoes (2 to 3 inches), such as creamers or fingerlings, unpeeled

2 tablespoons chopped fresh parsley for garnish

light entrées

indian summer risotto

This Italian rice dish is easy to prepare, but it does require a bit of time to cook. Serve it as a light vegetarian entrée, with a salad to start and a fruit dessert to finish, and you have yourself a party menu. I like to serve this at summer's end to bid goodbye to the best of the sunny season's bounty. When making a risotto such as this one, select superfino Arborio rice (which has plump, oval grains) that is high in amylopectin, a component of starch. It lends a creaminess to the finished risotto, which is accentuated by the slow addition of liquid and constant stirring. Another unique feature of Arborio rice is the firm central core it retains when cooked, giving it a distinctive al dente texture.

serves 6

1 In a large sauté pan, heat 2 tablespoons of the olive oil over medium-high heat. Add the onion and sauté until softened and lightly browned, about 4 minutes.

2 Reduce the heat to medium. Add the zucchini and sauté for 3 to 5 minutes, or until the squash is lightly browned and well coated with the oil. Add the bell pepper and sauté for another 3 minutes, or until slightly softened. Cover and cook for about 3 minutes more, or until the pepper begins to wilt, stirring once or twice. Uncover, increase the heat to medium-high, and cook until the liquid has evaporated, about 1 minute more. Season with salt and pepper, remove from the heat, and set aside.

3 In a medium saucepan, bring the broth and wine to a simmer on medium-high heat. (Or place in a large glass measuring cup and microwave on high for 2 minutes.)

¼ cup olive oil

1 large onion, finely chopped

1 pound yellow and green zucchini, cut into ½-inch dice

1 red or yellow bell pepper, seeded and cut into ½-inch dice

Salt and pinch of freshly ground black pepper

5 cups chicken or vegetable broth

½ cup dry white wine

1½ cups Arborio rice

2 tablespoons finely chopped fresh parsley, plus whole leaves for garnish

2 tablespoons finely chopped fresh basil, plus whole leaves for garnish

½ cup freshly grated Parmesan cheese, plus extra for serving

THE CLEVER COOK COULD:

- Add a cup of chopped yellow or red tomatoes in step 5.

- Try other cheeses like Asiago or Pecorino Toscano in place of the Parmesan.

- Add a tablespoon of mascarpone at the end to give the risotto a supercreamy, rich flavor.

- Add some Basic Vinaigrette (page 204) to any leftover risotto to make a rice salad.

4 In a large heavy saucepan, heat the remaining olive oil over medium heat. Add the rice and stir well, making sure that all the grains are well coated, about 2 minutes. Pour in ½ cup of the hot broth and stir, using a wooden spoon, until all of the broth is absorbed. Continue adding the broth, ½ cup at a time, making sure the rice has absorbed the broth before adding more, and stirring constantly so the rice doesn't burn or stick. (It takes 3 to 5 minutes for the rice to absorb each addition of broth.) The rice should become very creamy as you continue to add the broth.

5 When you add the last ½ cup of broth, add the vegetable mixture with it, reduce the heat to low, and cook for 2 minutes more. You may need to use a fork to mix the vegetables with the rice. Remove from the heat and add the chopped parsley, basil, and ½ cup Parmesan cheese and stir well to blend with the rice. Spoon into shallow serving bowls and garnish with the parsley and basil leaves before serving. Pass the extra Parmesan separately.

party prep

The risotto can be made through step 2 up to 4 hours ahead. Cover the vegetables and leave at room temperature.

spicy
mac & cheese
with caramelized leeks

Mac and cheese is a great vegetarian party dish. Just about everyone likes it. The combination of cheddar cheese, spicy pepper Jack, and a touch of Parmesan transforms this mac and cheese into a sophisticated dish. The caramelized leeks add another layer of flavor, in addition to the crispy bread-crumb topping. This recipe can easily be doubled for a larger gathering; just use a deep 9-x-13-inch baking dish.

serves 6

1 Preheat the oven to 375°F. Butter an 8-inch square or 9-x-11-inch baking dish.

2 To make the leeks: Heat the olive oil in a large nonreactive skillet over medium-high heat. Add the leeks and sauté, stirring frequently, for about 15 minutes, or until well softened and nicely caramelized. Season with salt and pepper. Transfer to a large bowl and set aside.

3 Bring a large pot of water to a rapid boil and add the salt. Add the macaroni and stir to separate. Cook over high heat until al dente, 5 to 7 minutes, stirring occasionally. Drain well. Put the macaroni in the bowl with the leeks and toss. Set aside.

4 To make the sauce: In a large saucepan over medium-low heat, melt the butter. Sprinkle the flour over the butter and whisk to mix well. Cook, stirring constantly, for about 2 minutes, or until the flour is absorbed and the mixture is bubbling gently and has turned golden. Add the milk gradually, stirring constantly, and bring the sauce to a simmer over medium heat. Continue to cook until the white sauce is smooth and slightly thickened, 3 to 4 minutes. Add the three cheeses. Remove from the heat and whisk until the cheese is completely melted. Stir in the salt, pepper, and mustard. Taste for seasoning. Pour the sauce over the macaroni-leek mixture and stir to coat the mixture evenly.

caramelized leeks

3 tablespoons olive oil

6 leeks, light green and white parts only, cleaned and finely chopped

Salt and freshly ground black pepper

1 tablespoon salt

3 cups large elbow macaroni (about ¾ pound)

sauce

3 tablespoons unsalted butter

3 tablespoons all-purpose or Wondra flour

3 cups warm milk or half-and-half

2 cups shredded pepper Jack cheese

2 cups shredded sharp cheddar cheese

¼ cup freshly grated Parmesan cheese

½ teaspoon salt

½ teaspoon freshly ground white pepper

1 tablespoon Dijon mustard

topping

½ cup bread crumbs, preferably Japanese panko crumbs

¼ cup freshly grated Parmesan cheese

2 tablespoons unsalted butter, cut into tiny pieces

5 Place the prepared baking dish on a baking sheet and transfer the macaroni mixture to the dish.

6 To make the topping: In a small bowl, combine the bread crumbs and Parmesan and mix well. Sprinkle over the macaroni in an even layer. Dot with the butter pieces.

7 Bake, uncovered, for 35 to 40 minutes, or until the top is bubbling and beginning to form a golden brown crust. Be very careful not to let the bread crumbs burn. Let stand for at least 10 minutes before serving.

party prep

The dish may be prepared through step 5 up to 2 days ahead, covered, and refrigerated. Bring to room temperature before baking. You can also bake the dish ahead of time and bring to room temperature. In that case, reheat in a 350°F oven for 20 minutes, or until hot throughout. You may need to cover it with aluminum foil so the top does not burn.

THE CLEVER COOK COULD:

- Add 1 cup cooked diced turkey or chicken before baking for a more substantial dish.

- Instead of pepper Jack and cheddar cheese, use 2 cups of grated Gruyère and 2 cups of freshly grated Parmesan cheese. Add a few teaspoons of white truffle oil to the cheese sauce after it has cooked. Or use white truffle butter instead of plain butter to dot the top of the casserole before baking.

- Add 1 cup each of frozen petits pois (small peas), defrosted, and sautéed sliced cremini mushrooms before baking.

baked greek pasta

When planning a menu for a party, remember that pasta casseroles often are a cook's best friend, and this one is no exception. It can be assembled ahead, refrigerated, and then baked in the oven shortly before you are ready to serve, leaving time before the party for other things. This adaptation of pastitsio, a Greek pasta dish, combines eggplant and lamb in a rustic tomato and wine sauce, scented with cinnamon and oregano. A Parmesan-flavored topping, enriched with some of the meat and tomato sauce, is spooned on top of the pasta, which gets a final sprinkling of Parmesan or pecorino cheese.

serves 8 to 10

1 To make the sauce: Put the eggplant in a colander over a sink or a bowl and sprinkle with a few teaspoons of salt. Let the juices drain for 15 minutes. This will remove any bitter taste from the eggplant. Wipe the eggplant dry with a paper towel.

2 In a large nonstick skillet, heat the olive oil over medium-high heat. Sauté the eggplant for about 5 minutes, or until softened and browned. Set aside in a medium bowl. Sauté the onion in the same skillet for 5 to 7 minutes, or until nicely softened. Add the lamb and brown it, breaking it up with a spoon, until no longer pink and all the liquid has evaporated, about 5 minutes. Add the wine and simmer until it has evaporated, 7 to 10 minutes. Add the oregano, cinnamon, marinara sauce, and cooked eggplant. Season with salt and pepper. Simmer over medium heat for about 5 minutes more, or until slightly reduced yet still soupy. Taste for seasoning and remove from the heat. (Measure out 1 cup of the sauce for the topping, and leave the rest in the skillet.)

3 To make the topping: Melt the butter in a medium saucepan over medium heat. Sprinkle in the flour and cook, stirring constantly, for 3 minutes. Slowly add the milk, and nutmeg, season with salt and pepper, and whisk the sauce until thickened and smooth, 4 to 5 minutes. Add the $\frac{1}{2}$ cup of Parmesan cheese and the 1 cup of reserved meat sauce and mix to combine. Cook the sauce for 2 minutes more, or until the cheese has melted. Taste for seasoning and set aside.

sauce

1 pound eggplant, peeled and cut into $\frac{1}{2}$-inch pieces

Salt

3 tablespoons olive oil

1 onion, finely chopped

1$\frac{1}{2}$ pounds ground lamb

1 cup dry red wine, such as Merlot or Cabernet Sauvignon

1$\frac{1}{2}$ teaspoons dried oregano

1 teaspoon ground cinnamon

Two 26-ounce jars best-quality marinara sauce

Freshly ground black pepper

topping

4 tablespoons unsalted butter

$\frac{1}{4}$ cup all-purpose flour

2 cups whole milk

Freshly grated nutmeg

Salt and freshly ground black pepper

$\frac{1}{2}$ cup freshly grated Parmesan cheese (or use a mix of half Pecorino Romano or Toscano and half Parmesan)

1 pound large elbow macaroni or small shells

$\frac{3}{4}$ cup freshly grated Parmesan cheese (or a mix of half Pecorino Romano or Toscano and half Parmesan)

2 tablespoons finely chopped fresh parsley for garnish

4 Preheat the oven to 350°F. Bring a large pot of salted water to a boil over high heat. Cook the pasta for about 8 minutes, or until al dente. Drain and transfer to a large bowl. Add the remaining meat and tomato sauce and mix together until well blended.

5 Grease a 9-x-13-inch baking dish. Transfer the mixture to the dish, making sure that the sauce is evenly distributed.

6 Spoon the tomato-flavored white sauce over the top of the pasta evenly. Sprinkle the ¾ cup Parmesan cheese over the pasta.

7 Bake for about 30 minutes, or until the dish is cooked through. Turn on the broiler. Place the dish on the upper rack and brown the topping for about 2 minutes. Watch carefully. Remove from the oven and sprinkle with parsley. Serve immediately.

party prep

The dish may be prepared through step 6 up to 1 day ahead, covered, and refrigerated. Remove from the refrigerator 2 hours before baking. You can also prepare this through step 2 up to 2 days ahead, cover the sauce, and refrigerate. Taste and adjust the seasonings.

THE CLEVER COOK COULD:

- Make this dish for vegetarians. Omit the lamb; increase the eggplant to 2 pounds, cut into larger pieces (1 inch); and, for extra flavor, increase the cinnamon to 1¼ teaspoons and the oregano to 2 teaspoons. Add 1 pound of fresh baby spinach leaves when you mix the sauce with the pasta; make sure they are evenly distributed.

penne
with roasted broccoli & pistachio gremolata

The lemon-scented gremolata transforms a basic pasta and broccoli dish into one you'll be proud to serve at any dinner party. It's equally delicious as a vegetarian main course or a side dish. Try it with duck or grilled chicken.

serves 6

1 To make the gremolata: Preheat the oven to 350°F. Spread out the pistachios on a baking sheet and toast for about 5 minutes, or until lightly browned and fragrant. (Leave the oven on.) Cool the pistachios, finely chop, and transfer to a small bowl. Add the lemon zest, garlic, and parsley. Mix well and set aside.

2 Raise the oven temperature to 425°F. Put the broccoli in a large shallow roasting pan or on a rimmed baking sheet, drizzle with 2 tablespoons of the olive oil, season with salt and pepper, and mix well. Make sure to coat the broccoli evenly with the oil, and keep it in a single layer.

3 Roast the broccoli for 20 to 25 minutes, or until crisp, lightly browned, and cooked through, stirring occasionally. Watch carefully so it doesn't burn. When the broccoli is cooked, sprinkle it with the lemon juice and stir to combine. Roast for 1 minute more. Remove from the heat and let cool slightly. Set aside.

4 Bring a large pot of generously salted water to a boil. Cook the pasta according to the package directions, or until al dente, 8 to 9 minutes. Drain the pasta, reserving 1 cup of the pasta water.

5 In a large serving bowl, combine the drained pasta with the broccoli and toss to blend well. Add the remaining 1 tablespoon olive oil, $1/3$ cup of the pasta water, and the gremolata. Season with salt and pepper and toss again until well combined. Add more pasta water if the mixture needs a bit more liquid. Serve immediately.

gremolata

¼ cup shelled raw pistachios

Zest of 1 large lemon

2 garlic cloves, minced

3 tablespoons finely chopped fresh parsley

1½ pounds broccoli, stems removed (about 1 pound 2-inch florets)

3 tablespoons olive oil

Salt and freshly ground black pepper

Juice of ½ lemon

1 pound penne

party prep

The dish may be prepared through step 3 up to 1 day ahead. Keep the gremolata covered and at room temperature. Cover and refrigerate the broccoli. Remove from the refrigerator 30 minutes before finishing the dish.

caramelized leek & asparagus crustless quiche

This springtime vegetable custard is colorful and lighter than the classic French quiche lorraine since it has no crust. You can find pencil-thin asparagus in the spring months. Bake this in a pretty quiche dish that you can bring to the table. Serve it with Roasted Tomato Jam (page 211) or Candied Bacon (page 147).

serves 6

1 Preheat the oven to 325°F. Trim the bottom third of the asparagus, and halve the asparagus crosswise. You should have about 4 cups. Set aside.

2 Heat the olive oil in a large sauté pan over medium heat. Add the leeks and sauté for 10 to 15 minutes, stirring occasionally, until lightly caramelized. Add the asparagus and sauté for 4 to 5 minutes, or until crisp-tender, stirring occasionally. The asparagus will turn bright green. Season with salt and pepper and let cool.

3 Combine the eggs, milk, both cheeses, flour, baking powder, 1 teaspoon salt, and a sprinkle of pepper in a medium bowl and whisk until completely blended.

4 Spread out the leek mixture evenly on the bottom of a greased 11-inch quiche dish. Pour the egg and cheese mixture over the vegetables.

5 Place the dish on a foil-lined baking sheet and bake for about 45 minutes, or until just firm. The center should be slightly jiggly.

6 Remove from the oven and let sit for 10 minutes. Cut into slices and serve immediately.

party prep

The quiche may be prepared through step 2 up to 1 day ahead, covered, and refrigerated. Preheat the oven while you continue with the recipe.

1 pound pencil-thin asparagus

¼ cup olive oil

5 leeks, light green and white parts only, cleaned and thinly sliced

Salt and freshly ground black pepper

6 large eggs

2 cups milk

½ cup grated Gruyère cheese

½ cup freshly grated Parmesan cheese

2 tablespoons all-purpose flour

1 teaspoon baking powder

deli frittata

As a child I often enjoyed deli omelets with my dad, which usually meant adding deli meats to the eggs. I reimagined that dish as a tasty egg pizza. I love making these flat, omelet-like pizzas, which can be as simple as adding some fresh herbs and cheese to beaten eggs, or as complicated as you would like. The tiny, marble-size potatoes will save you from the chore of cutting potatoes. This is great for brunch or a light supper.

serves 6 to 8

1 Preheat the oven to 425°F.

2 Drop the potatoes gently into a medium pan of boiling water and cook for 2 minutes. Drain the potatoes, let dry, and set aside.

3 Heat the olive oil in a 12-inch nonstick skillet with an ovenproof handle (or cover a wooden handle with foil) over medium-high heat. Add the leeks and sauté until soft but not brown, 5 to 6 minutes. Add the potatoes and cook, rolling them around, for 3 minutes, or until the potatoes are slightly tender. Add the chard, cover the pan, and steam for 3 to 4 minutes, or until the chard is wilted and the potatoes are tender. Add the salami and cook for 1 minute more. Season with salt and pepper.

4 Whisk the eggs in a medium bowl. Add the cheese, whisking until well blended, and season with salt and pepper.

5 Spread out the cooked vegetables and salami in the bottom of the skillet and pour the egg mixture over them. Cook over medium heat, stirring occasionally and lifting up the bottom with a spatula to allow more of the liquidy eggs to cook, until the bottom of the frittata is firm and lightly browned, about 5 minutes. The top will still be moist and slightly liquidy. Transfer the skillet to the oven and bake until the frittata is puffed and brown and the cheese is melted, about 10 minutes.

6 To make the drizzle: Combine the paprika, hot sauce, and olive oil in a small bowl and mix to blend.

7 Serve the frittata out of the pan or invert onto a large platter, placing a spatula underneath it to ensure it will slide out easily. Reinvert onto a serving platter, so the browned top faces up. Drizzle with the hot sauce and garnish with the parsley.

½ pound marble or baby red potatoes (about 1 inch in diameter; if larger, cut in half)

2 tablespoons olive oil

2 leeks, light green and white parts only, cleaned and thinly sliced

1 bunch red Swiss chard, stems removed, and coarsely shredded

3 ounces thinly sliced salami or prosciutto, cut into long strips

Salt and freshly ground black pepper

12 large eggs

1 cup shredded mozzarella or Manchego cheese

hot sauce drizzle

½ teaspoon paprika

1 teaspoon Sriracha hot sauce

1 teaspoon olive oil

2 tablespoons finely chopped fresh parsley for garnish

party prep

The frittata may be made up to 1 day ahead, covered, and refrigerated. Serve chilled, at room temperature, or reheat and serve warm.

THE CLEVER COOK COULD:

- Cut into bite-size squares and serve as an appetizer with cocktails.

- Drizzle some marinara sauce on top of the warm frittata and serve immediately.

light entrées

thyme & gruyère egg puffs with sautéed cherry tomato relish

These airy puffs of egg, thyme, and cheese are great for brunches when you don't want a lot of last-minute work. Fifteen minutes before you are ready to serve, pop these into muffin tins and watch them rise. So easy to make, these puffs taste even better with Sautéed Cherry Tomato Relish served alongside. Make up the relish ahead of time and just reheat before serving.

serves 6

1 Preheat the oven to 375°F. Crack the eggs into a medium bowl. Add the milk and beat together until the eggs are broken up and the milk is well incorporated. Add the baking powder, 1 cup of the cheese, the thyme, scallions, salt, and pepper. Stir the mixture and transfer to a large measuring cup or a bowl with a lip for easy pouring.

2 Grease the cups in a nonstick muffin tin with cooking spray. Pour some of the mixture into each cup, filling it about three-quarters full.

3 Bake for 9 minutes, or until slightly puffed. Sprinkle the remaining ¼ cup cheese over the tops. Bake for 3 to 5 minutes more, or until the eggs have puffed and are as soft or firm as you like them. Remove from the oven and let cool for 5 minutes before serving.

4 Reheat the tomato relish for 1 minute, until warmed through, and serve with the puffs.

party prep

The egg puffs may be prepared through step 2 up to 4 hours ahead, covered, and kept at room temperature.

12 large eggs

⅓ cup milk

½ teaspoon baking powder

1¼ cups grated Gruyère cheese

1 tablespoon finely chopped fresh thyme

4 scallions, light green and white parts only, finely chopped

¼ teaspoon salt

⅛ teaspoon freshly ground black pepper

Sautéed Cherry Tomato Relish (page 212)

italian picnic sandwich

This is my favorite summer sandwich. It's perfect to take on a boat, to the beach, or to a tailgate party. Make up your own signature picnic sandwich with some of your favorite fillings. The loaf is wrapped in butcher or parchment paper and tied off stylishly into individual sandwiches with raffia.

serves 8

1 Cut the baguette horizontally so that two-thirds of the bread is the bottom "half" and one-third is the top. Scoop out most of the soft bread inside, leaving the thick crust with only a thin layer of bread.

2 Brush some vinaigrette on the bottom half of the baguette. Top with the cucumber, tomato, basil, turkey, prosciutto, and artichoke hearts, distributing the ingredients evenly. Sprinkle with more vinaigrette and top with the cheese. Cover with the top half of the bread and press down firmly. Wrap in plastic wrap and refrigerate for at least 2 hours.

3 Remove the plastic wrap from the sandwich and wrap the loaf in butcher paper. Wrap twine or raffia tightly around the loaf at 2-inch intervals.

4 To serve, use a sharp, serrated knife to slice through the bread between the twine ties to make individual sandwiches.

party prep

The sandwich may be prepared up to 8 hours ahead, covered, and refrigerated. Take it out of the refrigerator 15 minutes before serving.

1 French or sourdough baguette

½ cup Basic Vinaigrette (page 204)

1 small European cucumber, peeled and thinly sliced

2 ripe tomatoes, thinly sliced

12 large fresh basil leaves

¼ pound thinly sliced roast turkey breast

¼ pound thinly sliced prosciutto

¾ cup marinated artichoke hearts, drained (one 6-ounce jar)

3 ounces fresh goat cheese, fresh mozzarella, or Burrata cheese, cut into bite-size pieces

THE CLEVER COOK COULD:

- Use cherry tomatoes and other fresh herbs in the winter, when tomatoes and fresh basil aren't in season.

- Vary the filling ingredients. Try including roasted red peppers, grilled eggplant or zucchini, or sun-dried tomatoes. Make sure to follow the suggested quantities above so you will have the proper ratio of ingredients to bread.

grilled flatbreads or pizzas
with caramelized onions, sausage & manchego cheese

What's the difference between a pizza and a flatbread? Mostly the shape and thickness. Pizzas are round and tend to be a bit thicker than flatbread. Flatbreads are shaped into rectangles or ovals and are rolled very thin, which gives them a crispy texture after baking. With this recipe, you can make either one.

Pizza is one of the easiest things to make. And you don't have to be a pizza tosser to make great pizza or flatbread. Use a rolling pin to guide the dough to its proper shape and thickness. If you are pressed for time, pick up some pizza dough at your favorite pizza place. They will be happy to sell you the dough. Or pick some up at the market. Remember that 1 pound of dough will make two large pizzas or flatbreads. You can serve this recipe as an appetizer or as a main dish, depending upon what else is on the menu. Try out different combinations of ingredients to find your own signature dish (see the suggestions on page 112). An outdoor grill with a lid is preferred for this dish. But you can also bake it in the oven.

serves 8

1 In a small skillet, heat the olive oil over medium heat. Add the sausage and brown for 6 to 7 minutes, breaking up the meat with a spatula as it cooks. Once cooked through and broken up into crumbles, remove from the heat and drain on paper towels. Set aside.

[recipe continues]

1 tablespoon olive oil

¾ pound chicken or turkey Italian sausage (about 4 links), casing removed

1 recipe Pizza Dough (page 113), or 1 pound fresh store-bought pizza dough

1½ cups shredded Manchego cheese

1 cup shredded mozzarella cheese

1 cup Caramelized Onions (page 215)

¼ cup torn fresh basil leaves

THE CLEVER COOK COULD:

- Add sautéed mushrooms to the flatbread or pizza.

- Substitute buffalo mozzarella or fresh goat cheese for the Manchego cheese.

- Make a vegetarian version with sliced tomatoes, grilled eggplant, Burrata cheese, and fresh thyme leaves.

- Make a sweet-and-savory version with Caramelized Onions, blue cheese, and prosciutto.

2 Lightly flour two rimless baking sheets. Divide purchased pizza dough in half (if using). Working with dough half at a time, roll out on lightly floured surface to a 12-x-8-inch oval or a 10-inch round. Transfer to baking sheets. Spray top of flatbreads with olive oil spray.

3 Heat the barbecue to medium-high heat. Make sure your barbecue has a lid and place all topping ingredients next to the grill.

4 Place the flatbreads on foil-lined baking sheets and spray each side with olive oil cooking spray. Transfer the flatbreads to the grill and grill for 1½ to 2 minutes or until the dough begins to puff and light grill marks appear on the bottom.

5 Using a large spatula, flip over the flatbreads or pizza rounds and move them to the coolest part of the grill. Spread each one evenly with a quarter of the cheeses, and half the sausage, onions, and basil. Top with the remaining cheese. Move them back to the center of the grill and cover for 3 minutes. Check and rotate them. Cover the grill and cook for another 2 to 3 minutes. Watch carefully so they do not burn on the bottom. The cheese should be completely melted and the crust should be crisp and lightly charred. Remove from the grill and let cool for 5 minutes before cutting with a pizza wheel. Serve immediately.

Alternatively, bake the flatbreads or pizza in the oven: Preheat the oven to 475°F. Place the crusts on perforated pizza pans. Poke the crust gently and evenly with a fork. Cook in the oven for 5 minutes, or until the crusts are lightly browned. Remove from the oven and spread evenly with the toppings. Return to the oven and cook for 10 minutes, or until the cheese is melted and lightly browned. Serve immediately.

PIZZA OR FLATBREAD TOPPINGS

Pizza topping combinations are a really fun way to be creative because it is hard to go wrong. Here are some ideas for inspiration, but play around with different options to build your ultimate pizza.

- For a savory white pizza, mozzarella and fresh goat cheese, sautéed leeks, sliced button mushrooms, and fresh thyme.

- Parmesan cheese and olive oil, topped with arugula and tomato salad with Parmesan shards.

- For a green pizza, basil pesto, mozzarella cheese, and spinach on top.

- For a Mexican-style pizza, red onion, roasted chiles, tomatoes, cheddar cheese, cilantro, and sliced avocado on top. Add seasoned ground beef or chorizo if you like.

- Sun-dried tomatoes, tomato sauce, diced chicken, and artichoke hearts.

- Grilled eggplant, tomato, Parmesan cheese, and thyme.

- Leftover Pulled Pork (page 144) and pepper Jack cheese.

seriously simple parties

pizza dough

Here is a great basic recipe for pizza dough, which combines two flours to give the dough a toothsome, chewy quality. Semolina flour—a yellow, coarse, hard durum wheat—adds a bit of texture to the dough. Bread flour has more gluten in it, which helps the dough rise and gives it a breadlike quality when baked.

Makes two 14-x-8-inch flatbreads or two 12-inch pizzas

1 Pour the warm water into a large measuring cup, stir in the yeast and olive oil, and let sit for a few minutes, or until the mixture starts to bubble. On a clean surface, mix together both flours and the salt and form a large well in the middle. Once the yeast is ready, pour it carefully into the well. Using a fork, slowly begin to bring the flour into the well to incorporate it. Continue this process until the center is no longer runny and then bring the rest of the dough together until well incorporated and smooth. You can also make the dough in the food processor by combining the wet and dry ingredients together and pulsing until smooth.

2 Transfer the dough to a large oiled bowl and cover with a warm damp cloth. Place the bowl in a warm room for about 1½ hours, or until the dough has doubled in size.

3 Remove the dough from the bowl and place on a flour-dusted surface. Knead with your hands to extract the air and divide the dough into two balls. Roll them out as described on the facing page or in the recipe of your choice.

4 The pizza dough may be made 1 day ahead, wrapped in plastic, and refrigerated. Roll out the dough just before cooking.

1¼ cups warm water (between 105 and 115°F)

One ¼-ounce packet active dry yeast

2 tablespoons olive oil

2½ cups white bread flour

1 cup semolina flour

2 teaspoons salt

seafood entrées

steamed mussels
with garlic, tomatoes
& fresh herbs

These mussels are delicious served with warm, crusty French bread or Herbed Garlic Cheese Bread. This is a great one-pot dish for a casual party. A touch of smoky fire-roasted tomatoes and fresh basil give these mollusks a Mediterranean accent.

You can now find farm-raised mussels that are cleaned and debearded. All you need to do is give them a good rinse and light scrubbing before cooking. My fishmonger always throws in a few extra mussels, in case some of them don't open after cooking.

You can use black mussels or the New Zealand Green Lip mussels for this recipe. Make sure to have an extra bowl for the discarded shells.

serves 8 to 10 as a first course or 6 as a main course

1 Heat the olive oil in a very large pot that will accommodate all the mussels over medium-high heat. Sauté the shallots until nicely softened, about 2 minutes. Add the garlic and cook for another 30 seconds.

2 Add the wine, broth, tomatoes, basil, 2 tablespoons of the parsley, and butter. Season with pepper and bring to a boil. Reduce the heat to medium and simmer the broth for 4 to 5 minutes, or until aromatic. Add the mussels and cover tightly. Hold the stockpot with both handles and shake the mussels so that they will cook evenly. Steam them until they open, about 5 minutes.

3 Spoon the mussels into large soup bowls, spoon some broth over them, and sprinkle with the remaining 2 tablespoons parsley. Serve immediately with the bread for dipping.

party prep
This dish can be prepared through step 2 up to 4 hours ahead, covered, and left at room temperature. Be sure to bring the broth to a boil before adding the mussels.

3 tablespoons olive oil

8 shallots, minced

4 garlic cloves, minced

2 cups dry white wine

1 cup vegetable or chicken broth

One 14½-ounce can fire-roasted diced tomatoes with their juice, or 1½ cups peeled and diced tomatoes

2 tablespoons finely chopped fresh basil

4 tablespoons finely chopped fresh parsley

4 tablespoons unsalted butter

Freshly ground black pepper

6 pounds mussels, well scrubbed

A crusty French baguette or Herbed Garlic Cheese Bread (page 59) for serving

THE CLEVER COOK COULD:

- Add more parsley or fresh chives, if fresh basil is unavailable.

- Add 1 cup of fresh bread crumbs to the broth when boiling to give the broth a thicker texture.

- Substitute littleneck clams for the mussels. Make sure that they are well scrubbed before cooking.

- Add ¼ cup of cream before adding the mussels or clams for a creamier dish.

seriously simple parties

roasted shrimp scampi provençal

For those days when you don't have much time, this dish is easy and quick, has big flavor, and a beautiful, rustic presentation—making it ideal for impromptu entertaining. Ask your fishmonger to peel and devein the shrimp, making sure to keep the tails attached. While it may cost a bit more, it is worth it because of the time you will save. Roasting the shrimp brings out its inherent sweetness. I've replaced the traditional butter sauce with tomatoes, garlic, wine, and herbs, which make this a lighter entrée that I know your guests will appreciate. You can serve this right from the baking dish, so use a pretty one that can come straight to the table. Or serve the shrimp in individual gratin dishes if you like. A simple vegetable rice pilaf or pasta with olive oil and garlic is a nice accompaniment.

serves 6

1 Preheat the oven to 425°F.

2 To make the sauce: Heat the olive oil in a large skillet over medium-high heat. Add the shallots and sauté for 2 minutes, or until softened. Add the garlic and sauté for 1 minute more, or until softened but not browned. Add the tomatoes, wine, and herbs; season with salt and pepper; bring to a simmer. Cook over medium heat for 3 to 5 minutes, or until the sauce is slightly thickened. Taste for seasoning.

3 Rinse and dry the shrimp. Put in a 14-inch round or a 13-inch square baking dish. Drizzle with the olive oil and wine and sprinkle with the seasoning salt and pepper. Toss with tongs to evenly coat. Arrange the shrimp in a single layer, cut-side down, with the tails facing in. Roast for about 6 minutes, or until partially cooked. Top with the sauce and bake for 8 minutes more, or until the shrimp are pink and opaque all the way through. Garnish with the parsley and serve immediately.

party prep

The sauce may be prepared up to 2 days ahead, covered, and refrigerated. Bring to room temperature before continuing with the recipe.

sauce

2 tablespoons olive oil

2 shallots, finely chopped

6 garlic cloves, minced

One 14½-ounce can fire-roasted crushed tomatoes

½ cup dry white wine

1 tablespoon finely chopped fresh parsley

1 tablespoon finely chopped fresh basil

Salt and freshly ground black pepper

2 pounds large shrimp (12 to 15 per pound), deveined and butterflied, with tails left on

3 tablespoons olive oil

2 tablespoons dry white wine

Seriously Simple Seasoning Salt (page 217) or store-bought seasoning salt

Freshly ground black pepper

2 tablespoons finely chopped fresh parsley for garnish

THE CLEVER COOK COULD:

- Drizzle the shrimp with an herbed pesto.

- Pour the shrimp and sauce over 1½ pounds of linguine, toss, and serve.

mexican seafood & scallion sauté
with mango-avocado salsa

I often marinate seafood, skewer it, and grill it. One day I decided to sauté marinated shrimp and scallops instead and the result was a very successful party dish. The remaining marinade reduces with the scallions and seafood in the pan, and it becomes a flavorful glaze. Make sure to reserve half of the marinade for making the glaze. The Mango-Avocado Salsa complements the Mexican flavors in the sauce. Serve warm corn tortillas alongside this spicy party dish.

serves 6

1 To make the marinade: Whisk together the lime juice, tequila, garlic, shallots, and cumin. Season with salt and pepper. Slowly add the olive oil, whisking until the ingredients are combined. Taste for seasoning.

2 Put the shrimp and scallops in separate lock-top plastic bags. Pour half of the marinade in one bag and the remaining half in the other. Move the seafood around to evenly coat each piece. Seal the bags and marinate for at least 30 minutes and up to 4 hours. Remove the seafood from the marinade and pat dry. Reserve the marinade.

3 In a very large skillet, heat 2 tablespoons of the olive oil over medium-high heat. Make sure the pan is very hot. Add the scallops and sauté, turning to cook evenly and brown, 3 to 5 minutes. Transfer to a platter. Heat the remaining 2 tablespoons oil, add the shrimp and scallions, and continue cooking, tossing constantly, until the scallions are soft and the shrimp is bright pink and cooked through, about 4 minutes. Add the cooked scallops and the reserved marinade from the plastic bags and bring to a boil. Cook for 1 minute more.

marinade

¼ cup fresh lime juice

¼ cup tequila

2 medium garlic cloves, minced

2 medium shallots, finely chopped

2 teaspoons ground cumin

Salt and freshly ground black pepper

⅓ cup olive oil

1½ pounds peeled and deveined jumbo shrimp (preferably 6 to 8 per pound)

1 pound medium to large sea scallops (10 to 20 per pound)

4 tablespoons olive oil

12 scallions, light green and white parts only, thinly sliced

Sliced limes for garnish

Mango-Avocado Salsa (recipe follows) for serving

Warm corn tortillas for serving

4 Spoon the seafood onto a platter and garnish with the limes. Serve with the salsa and warm tortillas on the side.

party prep

The dish may be prepared through step 2 up to 4 hours ahead, covered, and refrigerated.

mango-avocado salsa

Be sure to wear rubber gloves when chopping the jalapeño. You can also use canned jalapeños for this recipe if fresh are not available. Omit the lemon juice if using canned chiles.

makes about 1¼ cups

1 mango, peeled, pitted, and diced

1 large ripe avocado, peeled, pitted, and diced

1 jalapeño chile, seeded and finely chopped

1 shallot, finely chopped

2 tablespoons finely chopped fresh mint

2 tablespoons fresh lime juice

Salt

Combine the mango, avocado, jalapeño, shallot, mint, and lime juice in a medium mixing bowl and stir to combine. Season with salt. Refrigerate, covered, until ready to serve.

party prep

The salsa may be prepared up to 4 hours ahead, covered, and refrigerated.

THE CLEVER COOK COULD:

• Transform the salsa into a tropical guacamole. Omit the mint and mash the avocado. Serve the guacamole with crisp wonton skins, taro chips, or tortilla chips.

oven-baked paella

Paella makes a great dinner party centerpiece. A major plus for a party is that it can stay warm for up to 45 minutes after cooking. Although paella is usually cooked on top of the stove and requires a great deal of attention, this version is baked in the oven. That leaves the host with more time to make last-minute preparations—or have a relaxing glass of wine before the guests arrive! This one-dish main course needs only a salad like Arugula Salad with Roasted Grapes (page 87) or a soup like White Gazpacho (page 76) to begin. A refreshing trio of sorbets or a simple caramel flan would be a lovely dessert.

serves 6 to 8

1 Preheat the oven to 350°F. Heat the olive oil over medium-high heat in a 14-inch paella pan or 13- or 14-inch ovenproof sauté pan. Sauté the onions until softened, about 7 minutes. Add the bell pepper and sauté for about 2 minutes, or until slightly softened. Add the chorizo and sauté for about 2 minutes, or until well coated with the oil. Stir in the garlic and cook for 30 seconds. Add the tomato paste and paprika and cook about 1 minute, until slightly darker in color. Season with salt and pepper.

2 Add the rice and cook for 1 minute, stirring to coat the rice without browning it. Pour in the clam juice and 1 cup of the broth, and, using pot holders, move the pan around so that the ingredients are in an even layer and are mixed together. Cook until the liquid is absorbed, 4 to 5 minutes.

3 Add the rest of the broth and the saffron and bring to a boil. Cover and put in the oven. (If you don't have a cover, use aluminum foil.) Bake for 30 to 35 minutes, or until the liquid is almost absorbed.

[recipe continues]

3 tablespoons olive oil

2 medium onions, finely chopped

1 red bell pepper, seeded and cut into ½-inch dice

¼ pound Spanish chorizo, thinly sliced and cut into ½-inch dice

2 garlic cloves, minced

1 tablespoon tomato paste

1¼ teaspoons smoked paprika

Salt and freshly ground black pepper

1 pound medium-grain rice, preferably bomba or Arborio

1 cup clam juice

6 cups fish or chicken broth

1 teaspoon saffron threads

1 pound mussels or littleneck clams, or a combination of the two, well scrubbed

1 pound jumbo shrimp, peeled and deveined

1 pound precooked chicken or turkey sausage, sliced ½ inch thick

1½ cups frozen petite peas

2 tablespoons chopped fresh parsley for garnish

4 Remove the pan from the oven and add the shellfish, sausage, and peas and stir to blend well. Cover, return to the oven, and cook for 10 to 15 minutes, or until the mussels or clams are open and the shrimp are pink and fully cooked. Remove from the oven and keep covered until serving. (Discard any mussels or clams that have not opened.) Garnish with the parsley just before serving.

party prep

The paella may be prepared up to 45 minutes before serving. Cover to keep warm.

THE CLEVER COOK COULD:

- Use boneless chicken thighs instead of the sausage. Brown the thighs and then add to the paella in step 4, along with the shellfish and peas.

- Add some Basic Vinaigrette (page 204) to any leftover paella and serve chilled as a paella salad.

PAELLA TIPS

You will need the following to make your paella a success:

- A medium-grain rice like Spanish bomba rice or Italian Arborio. (The goal is for the rice to absorb the liquid and stay relatively firm.)

- Saffron threads, not powder.

- A lightweight paella pan 13 inches in diameter, so the rice will cook in a thin layer, encouraging lots of flavor and a crisp crust on the bottom. If you don't have a paella pan, use a 13- or 14-inch ovenproof skillet. (Avoid cast iron because it becomes too hot, and nonstick because it does not form a crust well.)

ahi burgers
with ginger-sesame mayonnaise

Fresh tuna has become a staple at most supermarkets. Try to select fillets that are very fresh and don't have blood lines running through them. Here, the tuna is finely chopped in the food processor with plenty of garlic and fresh basil. Once the patties are chilled and firm, they are grilled until medium. Make sure they are not overcooked, or they will be dry. I always serve these along with beef burgers so guests have a choice.

serves 4

1 To make the burgers: In a food processor, mince the garlic. Add the tuna, olive oil, basil, anchovy paste, and pepper and pulse until the mixture resembles the texture of ground meat. Divide the mixture into four balls and form them into 1-inch-thick patties. Place on a wax paper–lined baking sheet. Cover and refrigerate for at least 30 minutes.

2 To make the mayonnaise: In a small bowl, stir together the mayonnaise, sesame seeds, sesame oil, vinegar, and ginger. Season with the hot pepper sauce. Cover and refrigerate until ready to use.

3 Coat a perforated grill sheet pan with nonstick cooking spray and put it on the grill. Preheat the grill to medium-high. Put the tuna patties on the sheet pan and cook for about 2 minutes on each side for medium.

4 To serve, place the lettuce leaves on the bottoms of the buns. Top with the burgers and about 1 tablespoon of the mayonnaise. Cover with the bun tops.

party prep
The burgers and mayonnaise may be prepared through step 2 up to 6 hours ahead. Keep them covered and refrigerated.

burgers

4 garlic cloves, peeled

1¾ pounds fresh, well-chilled tuna fillets, trimmed of any dark spots and cut into large chunks

3 tablespoons olive oil

¼ cup chopped fresh basil

2 teaspoons anchovy paste

½ teaspoon freshly ground black pepper

ginger-sesame mayonnaise

½ cup mayonnaise

1½ teaspoons toasted sesame seeds

½ teaspoon sesame oil

½ teaspoon Champagne vinegar or white wine vinegar

1 teaspoon finely chopped pickled ginger

Dash of hot pepper sauce, such as Sriracha

4 medium crisp butterhead or romaine lettuce leaves for serving

4 brioche or soft hamburger buns, toasted, for serving

THE CLEVER COOK COULD:

• Sauté the burgers in a large skillet over medium-high heat.

• Make these into 1½-inch sliders with mini-buns or slider rolls.

seafood entrées

grilled sea bass
with basil-mint sauce

Easy to prepare, these flavor-packed marinated fish fillets are great for casual dinner parties. With the addition of yogurt, some of the marinade becomes a lovely quick sauce. Make up the marinade and sauce in the morning, and later on the fish will marinate and cook in no time. You'll find this zesty marinade is also great on other types of fish or on chicken.

serves 4 to 6

1 To make the marinade: In a small food processor, combine the ginger, mint, basil, honey, vinegar, and vegetable oil. Season with salt and pepper and pulse until smooth, but with small bits of herbs still visible.

2 In a small bowl, mix ½ cup of the marinade with the yogurt to serve as a dipping sauce on the side. Cover and refrigerate the sauce until ready to serve.

3 Put the fish fillets in a large lock-top plastic bag. Add the remaining marinade, press out the air, and seal the bag. Turn to coat the fish with the marinade and refrigerate for at least 30 minutes, or up to 2 hours.

4 Preheat the grill to medium-high. Remove the sea bass from the marinade and grill until the fish is cooked through and opaque, 3 to 5 minutes per side, depending on the thickness of the fillets. Remove from the heat and place on a serving platter. Serve immediately with the sauce on the side.

party prep
The dish may be prepared through step 2 up to 8 hours ahead. Refrigerate the marinating fish.

marinade

1 tablespoon chopped peeled fresh ginger

⅓ cup packed fresh mint leaves

⅓ cup packed fresh basil leaves

1½ tablespoons honey

¼ cup rice wine vinegar

½ cup vegetable oil

Salt and freshly ground black pepper

½ cup plain nonfat yogurt

4 to 6 half-pound sea bass fillets, checked for bones

THE CLEVER COOK COULD:

- **Make extra marinade and combine it with some yogurt and mayonnaise for a vegetable dip.**

- **Try this with salmon, swordfish, or halibut.**

seriously simple parties

roasted halibut
with mint pea purée

I like to serve this in shallow soup bowls for a pretty presentation. For a colorful finish, garnish with Sautéed Cherry Tomato Relish (page 212) or a dollop of Roasted Tomato Jam (page 211).

serves 6

1 To make the pea purée: Heat the olive oil in a large saucepan over medium heat. Sauté the shallots for about 4 minutes, or until nicely softened. Add the garlic and cook for 30 seconds. Add the peas and the broth and bring to a simmer. Cover and cook for 4 to 5 minutes, or until the peas are cooked through. Remove from the heat.

2 Purée the peas with an immersion blender, leaving some texture and making sure that some peas remain whole. Stir in the mint, lemon zest, and crème fraîche. Season with salt and pepper and set aside.

3 In a medium bowl, combine the panko, herbs, and lemon zest. Season with salt and pepper, mix well, and set aside.

4 Preheat the oven to 350°F. Place the fish pieces on wax paper. Generously coat all sides of the fish with cooking spray. Sprinkle the bread crumb and herb mixture onto one side of the fish and pat it so the coating adheres. Flip the fish and repeat on the other side. Line a baking sheet with foil, put a cake rack on the baking sheet, and place the fish on the rack. Sprinkle any remaining bread crumb mixture on top of the fish.

5 Roast the fish until flaky, 15 to 25 minutes, depending upon the thickness. To crisp the top, turn the oven to broil and place the fish under the broiler for 1 to 2 minutes.

6 Spoon about ½ cup of the pea purée onto each dinner plate and place the fish on top. Garnish with a slice of lemon before serving.

party prep

The fish and pea purée may be prepared 4 hours in advance through step 4, covered, and refrigerated.

pea purée

2 tablespoons olive oil

2 shallots, chopped

2 garlic cloves, minced

1½ pounds frozen petits pois (small peas), defrosted

1½ cups vegetable or chicken broth

1 tablespoon plus 1 teaspoon finely chopped fresh mint

Zest of 1 lemon

2 tablespoons crème fraîche or sour cream

Salt and freshly ground black pepper

¾ cup panko (Japanese-style bread crumbs)

¼ cup minced fresh parsley

2 tablespoons finely chopped mint

Zest of 1 lemon

Salt and freshly ground white pepper

Six 1 pound center-cut pieces of halibut fillets, about 1½ inches thick

Olive oil cooking spray

Lemon wedges for garnish

THE CLEVER COOK COULD:

- **Use leftover pea purée to make pea soup by adding additional chicken or vegetable broth until desired texture is reached.**

- **Use salmon, sea bass, or monkfish instead of the halibut.**

whole slow-roasted salmon
with sweet mustard–dill aioli

For years I would prepare cold salmon only one way—by poaching it. Once I discovered the virtues of slow roasting salmon, I never looked back. You'll find that this cooking technique gives salmon a creamy, moist texture. You can serve this warm or chilled. When chilled, the salmon makes a refreshing summertime main course. The sweet mustard–dill sauce is a re-creation of the Konditori dill sauce that I enjoyed on open-faced sandwiches and cold salmon when I was growing up.

serves 6 as a main course and up to 12 for a large buffet with other dishes

1 To make the aioli: Combine the mayonnaise, garlic, mustard, vinegar, and dill in a small serving bowl. Season with salt and pepper and mix to blend. Taste for seasoning and chill until serving.

2 Preheat the oven to 275°F. Rub both sides of the salmon with the seasoning salt and olive oil, and sprinkle with the lemon juice.

3 Place the salmon, skin-side down, on a nonstick or foil-lined baking sheet. Roast for 26 to 32 minutes, depending on the thickness, until flaky and just cooked through. The salmon will appear very moist. If serving cold, let the salmon cool in the pan.

4 Transfer the salmon in one piece to a serving platter using spatulas. Or cut the salmon into serving pieces and arrange on a platter. Either way, garnish with parsley and lemon slices.

party prep
The salmon can be cooked and refrigerated up to 1 day before serving. The sauce can be prepared, covered, and refrigerated for up to 3 days before serving.

sweet mustard–dill aioli

1 cup mayonnaise

2 garlic cloves, minced

¼ cup honey mustard

1 tablespoon good-quality white wine vinegar

2 tablespoons finely chopped fresh dill weed

Salt and freshly ground white pepper

One 3-pound salmon fillet, skin removed

Salt and freshly ground black pepper or Seriously Simple Seasoning Salt (page 217) or store-bought seasoning salt

1 tablespoon olive oil

Juice of ½ lemon

Fresh parsley sprigs for garnish

1 lemon, thinly sliced, for garnish

THE CLEVER COOK COULD:

* Add ½ cup of chopped European cucumber to the aioli.

* Replace the mayonnaise in the aioli with ½ cup of light mayonnaise and ½ cup of yogurt to lighten it up.

* Replace the aioli with Buttermilk Garden Herb Dressing (page 205).

seafood entrées

poultry entrées

grilled chicken
with green bean, sweet pepper & tomato salad & romesco sauce

I first tasted this "ode to summer" dish at Spruce restaurant in San Francisco. The chicken was beautifully presented on a bed of green bean and tomato salad, with a drizzle of earthy, sweet, yet slightly bitter romesco sauce. This is a one-dish meal and, with advance planning, it's easy for beginning cooks. Have your butcher split and flatten the chickens. Be sure to make the romesco sauce and salad before you cook the chicken. You can grill or roast these juicy chickens with equally excellent results.

serves 6

1 Put the flattened chicken on a baking sheet.

2 To make the marinade: In a small bowl, combine the seasoning salt, lemon zest and juice, and olive oil and stir to blend. Rub the mixture over the chickens so they are evenly covered. Put them in a large lock-top plastic bag and marinate for at least 30 minutes and up to 4 hours in the refrigerator.

3 Preheat a grill to medium-high. Grill the chicken, skin-side down, for about 7 minutes, or until the skin is crispy and brown. Turn over the chicken pieces, cover the grill, and continue cooking for 10 to 12 minutes, or until the chicken is cooked through and the juices run clear when the meat is pierced with a knife.

4 Spread out the green bean salad on a serving platter to make a bed. Place the chicken pieces on top of the salad. Drizzle 1 tablespoon romesco sauce over each piece of chicken. Serve immediately, with the remaining sauce on the side. You could also serve this on individual plates.

party prep
The chicken may be marinated 4 hours ahead, covered, and refrigerated.

3 small broiler chickens (about 2½ to 3 pounds each), split, backbone removed, and lightly flattened

marinade

2½ tablespoons Seriously Simple Seasoning Salt (page 217) or store-bought seasoning salt

Zest of 2 lemons

Juice of 1½ lemons

3 tablespoons olive oil

Green Bean, Sweet Pepper & Tomato Salad (page 91)

1 recipe Romesco Sauce (page 213)

THE CLEVER COOK COULD:

• Roast the chicken. Preheat the oven to 400°F. In a large nonstick ovenproof skillet, heat 3 tablespoons of oil over medium-high heat. Cook the chicken halves, skin-side down for about 5 minutes, or until the skin is crisp and brown. Turn the chicken over and place in the oven for 20 to 22 minutes, or until the chicken is cooked through and the juices run clear when the meat is pierced with a knife. Loosely cover the top with foil to avoid burning the skin.

sweet & spicy orange-hoisin chicken

Whether you serve it at a casual party for your family or a more formal dinner party, this will be a hit every time. The hoisin-flavored pan juices are reduced to a shiny glaze and drizzled on the chicken pieces, while the caramelized orange slices become a tasty garnish.

serves 8

1 To make the marinade: Combine all the ingredients except the marmalade and orange slices in a large nonreactive bowl. Add the marmalade and whisk the marinade to blend well. Taste for seasoning. Add the orange slices.

2 Put the chicken pieces into a large lock-top plastic bag. Pour in the marinade and coat all the pieces evenly. Press out the air, seal the bag, and marinate the chicken for at least 30 minutes and up to 4 hours in the refrigerator, turning it once or twice.

3 Preheat the oven to 425°F. Place the chicken pieces, skin-side up, in a large shallow roasting pan along with the marinade and orange slices and roast for 35 to 45 minutes, or until the chicken is golden brown and the juices run clear when the meat is pierced with a knife. Baste with the juices once or twice while it is roasting.

4 Remove the chicken from the pan and degrease the juices. Transfer the juices and cooked orange slices to a small saucepan over high heat, and reduce to a thin glaze, 6 to 8 minutes.

5 Arrange the chicken on a large serving platter, spoon the sauce over it, and garnish with the scallions and fresh orange slices. Serve immediately.

party prep
The dish may be prepared 1 day ahead, refrigerated, and served chilled. Or prepare it up to 2 hours ahead through step 2 and refrigerate.

marinade

¼ cup thinly sliced scallions, light green and white parts only

Zest and juice of 1 orange

½ cup hoisin sauce

1½ teaspoons chile paste with garlic or Sriracha hot sauce, or to taste

⅓ cup low-sodium soy sauce

1 tablespoon agave syrup

1 tablespoon rice wine vinegar

1 tablespoon dark sesame oil

2 tablespoons finely chopped peeled fresh ginger

⅓ cup orange marmalade

1 orange, thinly sliced

8 large bone-in chicken breast halves or assorted chicken pieces (about 6 pounds total)

2 tablespoons finely chopped scallions, green and white parts only, for garnish

1 orange, thinly sliced, for garnish

sautéed
chicken breasts
with port mushroom sauce

This is a very easy dish to make for a dinner party. Just be sure not to overcook the chicken. The touch of soy brings out the deep mushroom flavor of the sauce. I like to serve this with roasted baby potatoes or rice pilaf and sautéed mixed vegetables.

serves 6

1   In a large sauté pan, heat the 2 tablespoons of olive oil over medium-high heat. Season the chicken with seasoning salt. In batches, sauté the chicken for about 2 minutes, or until browned, and turn over with tongs. Continue cooking until the second side is browned and the chicken is just cooked through, another 2 to 3 minutes depending upon its thickness. Put the chicken on a platter and cover with foil.

2   Add the remaining ¼ cup of olive oil to the skillet. Sauté the mushrooms for about 5 minutes, or until nicely browned. Add the leeks and sauté, stirring frequently, for about 5 minutes, or until softened. Add the port, broth, soy sauce, and garlic and bring to boil, scraping up the browned bits on the bottom of the pan. Continue boiling until the liquid is slightly reduced and no alcohol remains, about 2 minutes.

3   Whisk in the crème fraîche and bring to a boil. Cook until slightly thickened, about 2 minutes. Add the tarragon and chives, season with salt and pepper, and whisk well. Taste for seasoning.

4   Return the chicken with its accumulated juices to the skillet, and cook for about 2 minutes more, or just until warmed through (be careful not to overcook). Arrange the chicken on a platter, spoon the sauce on top, and garnish with the parsley. Serve immediately.

party prep
The dish can be made through step 3 up to 2 hours ahead. Cover the sauce and chicken separately. Keep the sauce at room temperature and refrigerate the chicken. Remove 30 minutes before reheating.

2 tablespoons olive oil, plus ¼ cup

6 skinless, boneless chicken breast halves (about ⅓ to ½ pound each), lightly pounded until about ½ inch thick

Seriously Simple Seasoning Salt (page 217) or store-bought seasoning salt

1 pound cremini mushrooms, sliced

2 medium leeks, light green and white parts only, cleaned and finely chopped

½ cup tawny port

1¼ cups chicken broth

1 teaspoon soy sauce

2 medium garlic cloves, minced

2 tablespoons crème fraîche or whipping cream

1 tablespoon finely chopped fresh tarragon

2 tablespoons finely chopped fresh chives

Salt and freshly ground black pepper

2 tablespoons finely chopped fresh parsley or chives for garnish

grilled chicken breasts with herbed green sauce

I like to bring this dish to outdoor concert events. A zesty citrus marinade amps up the moistness of the chicken, which is complemented by the herbed green sauce. Serve the breast halves whole or sliced. They look pretty sliced on the bias with a drizzle of the cool, tangy sauce, which takes only a few minutes to prepare. Accompany this with the Green Bean, Sweet Pepper & Tomato Salad (page 91) or the Orzo Vegetable Salad (page 94) for a festive menu.

serves 6

1 To make the marinade: Combine the garlic, shallot, and lemon juice and zest in a small bowl and mix to blend. Add the olive oil and blend completely. Season with salt and pepper.

2 Put the chicken pieces in a large lock-top plastic bag and pour the marinade over the chicken; make sure the pieces are all evenly coated. Press out the air, close the bag, and refrigerate for 2 to 4 hours.

3 To make the sauce: Put the shallot, garlic, and lemon zest in a food processor and pulse five times, making sure it does not become a paste. Add the parsley and 2 tablespoons of the cornichons and pulse five times. Add the lemon juice and olive oil and pulse five more times. Be careful not to purée the mixture. Transfer the sauce to a small mixing bowl. Stir in the capers and remaining 2 tablespoons chopped cornichons. Season with salt and pepper.

marinade

1 medium garlic clove, minced

1 medium shallot, finely chopped

2 tablespoons fresh lemon juice

2 teaspoons minced lemon zest

¼ cup olive oil

Salt and freshly ground black pepper

6 boned chicken breast halves, with the skin left on (about ½ to ¾ pound each)

sauce

1 medium shallot, finely chopped

1 medium garlic clove, minced

1 teaspoon finely chopped lemon zest

¼ cup finely chopped fresh parsley leaves

¼ cup chopped fresh cornichons (sour gherkins)

¼ cup fresh lemon juice

¼ cup plus 2 tablespoons extra-virgin olive oil

1 tablespoon capers, drained and finely chopped

Salt and freshly ground black pepper

4 Preheat the grill to medium-high. Remove the chicken from the marinade. Grill the chicken about 3 inches from the heat for 6 to 8 minutes per side, or until no longer pink.

5 Place the chicken pieces on a serving platter and spoon some of the herbed green sauce on top of each breast. You can serve this at room temperature or right off the grill.

party prep

The sauce may be prepared 1 day ahead, covered, and left at room temperature. The chicken may be grilled 1 day ahead and served chilled.

- Cut the breasts into bite-size pieces and serve as an appetizer. Provide toothpicks and serve the sauce on the side.

- Make a chicken salad with leftover chicken. Combine the chopped chicken with spring greens, cherry tomatoes, olives, and garlic croutons. Add a few tablespoons of the sauce to Basic Vinaigrette (page 204) and toss with the salad.

braised
chicken thighs
with red wine & wild mushrooms

Chicken thighs are a good choice for a party dish. In this version of coq au vin, a French classic, smoky bacon and earthy dried wild mushrooms enhance the red wine sauce. The thighs are roasted separately and then incorporated into the sauce for the final braising, which keeps the thighs from overcooking. Consider this dish for a fall or winter dinner party when you're short on time, since you can make it a couple of days ahead and just reheat it.

serves 6 to 8

1 Put the mushrooms in a heat-proof bowl and pour the boiling water over them to cover. Let soften for at least 30 minutes. Strain the soaking liquid and reserve 1½ cups. Chop the mushrooms finely and reserve.

2 Preheat the oven to 450°F. Put the chicken thighs on a large baking sheet. Rub the olive oil on the thighs and sprinkle evenly with the seasoning salt and pepper. Roast the chicken for about 18 minutes, or until lightly golden. Leave the chicken on the baking sheet and set aside.

3 Put the bacon pieces in a deep sauté pan large enough to hold the chicken. Sauté over medium-high heat, turning them to cook evenly, 6 to 8 minutes, or until very crisp and brown. Remove with a slotted spoon and drain on paper towels. Set aside.

4 Pour off all but 3 tablespoons of the bacon fat and add the leeks to the pan. Cook, stirring occasionally, for about 8 minutes, or until softened. Add the carrots and cook for 2 minutes, or until slightly softened. Add the garlic and cook for 1 minute more. Add the red wine and the reserved strained mushroom liquid, the tomato paste, and thyme. Season with salt and pepper and bring to a boil over medium-high heat.

1½ ounces dried wild mushrooms

4 cups boiling water

4½ pounds skinless, boneless chicken thighs (about 16)

2 tablespoons olive oil

Seriously Simple Seasoning Salt (page 217) or store-bought seasoning salt

Freshly ground black pepper

6 applewood-smoked bacon strips (about ¼ pound), cut into 1-inch pieces

6 medium leeks, light green and white parts only, cleaned and sliced

2 carrots, peeled and thinly sliced

4 garlic cloves, minced

1 cup full-bodied red wine, such as Merlot, Cabernet Sauvignon, or Zinfandel

1 teaspoon tomato paste

¼ teaspoon dried thyme

Salt

2 tablespoons balsamic vinegar

4 tablespoons finely chopped fresh parsley.

5 Decrease the heat to medium-low and add the reserved mushrooms and the pan juices from the cooked chicken, and simmer for 5 minutes. Put the chicken in the pan and turn it to coat completely with the wine sauce. Cover and braise over low heat for about 15 minutes, or until the juices run clear when the chicken is pierced with a knife.

6 Add the balsamic vinegar to the sauce, raise the heat to medium-high, and boil down for 1 minute. Add the reserved bacon and 2 tablespoons of the parsley. Arrange the chicken pieces attractively on a platter. Spoon the sauce over the top and garnish with the remaining 2 tablespoons parsley. Serve immediately.

party prep

This dish may be made 2 days ahead, covered, and refrigerated. It also can be frozen. Defrost and bring to room temperature. Reheat the chicken in a 350°F oven for 20 minutes, or until hot and cooked through. Taste for seasoning.

butterflied dry-brined roast turkey
with maple butter

Turkey is a wonderful main course dish for a party, not just for Thanksgiving but for other occasions as well. Since the turkey is butterflied, it looks prettiest carved and arranged on a platter for serving. All the carving is done in the kitchen, another plus for party planning. The secret to this juicy turkey is to dry brine it, which means coating the bird with a seasoning salt and letting it rest in a sealed plastic bag for 3 days. When I tested this recipe, the turkey exceeded my expectations. It is highly flavorful, with firm meat and crisp skin. And best of all, because it's butterflied, there is less cooking time. You can butterfly the turkey yourself or have the butcher do it for you.

An instant-read thermometer is a must to ensure a perfectly cooked bird. Know that the temperature will increase a few degrees while the turkey rests. This is also excellent served cold, and you won't need to make the gravy.

serves 10 to 14

1 To make the rub: Three days before you cook the turkey, combine the lemon zest, thyme, and seasoning salt in a small bowl and mix to combine.

2 Wash the turkey inside and out and pat dry all over. Place the butterflied turkey, skin-side down, on a sheet of foil or the rack of a roasting pan. Rub a tablespoon or so of the salt mixture all over the bird, making sure the meat is well coated. Turn the bird over, skin-side up, and rub the remaining salt mixture all over the bird, concentrating on the breast and thigh areas. Put the bird in a 2½-gallon lock-top plastic bag and seal carefully. Refrigerate, turning every 12 hours and rubbing the salt in to coat it evenly, for 3 days.

rub
Zest of 1 lemon

2 tablespoons chopped fresh thyme, or 2 teaspoons dried

3 tablespoons Seriously Simple Seasoning Salt (page 217) or store-bought seasoning salt

One 14- to 16-pound turkey, butterflied (see facing page) and patted dry

2 onions, sliced

2 carrots, peeled and sliced

2 apples, peeled, cored, and sliced

1 cup chicken or turkey broth

½ cup (1 stick) unsalted butter, melted

2 tablespoons maple syrup

1 teaspoon soy sauce

gravy
½ cup (1 stick) unsalted butter

½ cup all-purpose flour

4 cups turkey or chicken broth

½ cup apple brandy

Salt and freshly ground black pepper

3 On the morning of the day you are going to cook the turkey, remove the turkey from the bag and place it, breast-side up, on a large rimmed jelly-roll pan. Pat the outside dry and refrigerate for at least 4 hours to help the skin dry further. Remove the turkey 1 hour before roasting to bring to room temperature.

4 Preheat the oven to 425°F. Tuck the onions, carrots, and apple slices underneath the turkey in an even layer. Pour the broth evenly on the bottom of the pan. Combine the melted butter with the maple syrup and soy sauce in a small bowl. Brush the turkey with the basting mixture.

5 Place the turkey in the center of the oven and roast for 30 minutes. Reduce the oven temperature to 350°F and roast for 1 hour more, basting occasionally with the accumulated pan juices and melted butter mixture. Reduce the heat to 325°F and roast for about 1 hour more, or until an instant-read thermometer inserted into the thickest part of the thigh, without touching bone, registers 170°F and the juices run clear. You may need to add more broth if the pan becomes too dry during roasting. If the bird is becoming too dark, place a tented piece of aluminum foil loosely on top. A 14- to 16-pound turkey should take a total cooking time of about 2½ hours; be sure to check the temperature at 30-minute intervals as the finish time approaches.

6 Remove the turkey from the oven and, with two large spatulas, transfer it to a large carving board. Discard the vegetables and pour the drippings into a fat separator for the gravy. Cover the turkey lightly with foil, and let the turkey rest for at least 20 minutes before carving.

7 To make the gravy: Melt the butter over medium-high heat and add the flour, whisking until blended. Cook the roux for about 5 minutes, or until nicely browned. Add the broth and the defatted drippings and cook for about 3 minutes, or until the gravy is slightly thickened. Add the apple brandy and cook for another 5 minutes, or until the gravy loses its floury taste. Season with salt and pepper.

8 Carve the turkey and arrange on a large platter. Serve the gravy on the side.

party prep

Dry-brine the bird 3 days ahead and refrigerate. Remove the turkey from the refrigerator 1 hour before roasting.

THE CLEVER COOK COULD:

- Use the rub on a 3½- to 4-pound whole chicken. Roast for about 1 hour at 425°F, covering it with foil if the bird becomes too brown.

- Gently stuff the bird under its skin with your favorite stuffing mixture.

- Serve the turkey chilled. Slice the breast, cut the other parts into serving pieces, and serve on a large platter.

- Keep the bones and use for making turkey soup.

HOW TO BUTTERFLY A TURKEY

- Put the turkey on a cutting board, breast-side down. Using poultry shears or a chef's knife, cut along both sides of the backbone, removing a strip about 2 inches wide. Refrigerate the bone for making turkey broth or soup.

- You should have one long turkey piece. Turn the turkey over and with the heel of your hand, press down firmly on the breastbone to crack it. The goal is to have a flat bird.

poultry entrées

crispy duck breast
with cherry port sauce

The key to the duck's crisp skin is letting it dry out overnight in the refrigerator, so start this the day before you plan to serve it. Quick to put together and much less messy than roasting a whole duck, the breasts are a perfect main course for a small dinner party. You and your guests can gather in the kitchen as you cook them up. This recipe will serve 4 to 6, depending upon how large the duck breasts are and how big your guests' appetites are. Try to find fresh duck breasts because the frozen variety tend to become rubbery. Muscovy or Hudson Valley ducks are preferable.

serves 4 to 6

1 Pound the duck halves between two pieces of wax paper with a heavy pan or a mallet to even out the thickness. (Or have your butcher do it.) Score the skin with a very sharp knife by cutting crisscrossing lines on it, making sure not to cut into the duck meat. Place the breasts on a baking sheet and cover loosely with wax paper. Refrigerate overnight to allow the skin to dry out.

2 In a skillet large enough to hold the 4 breast halves, melt the butter over medium-high heat. Sauté the duck breasts, skin-side down, for 5 to 7 minutes, or until the skin is very crisp and nicely browned. Turn over and sauté for another 5 minutes, or until the duck breasts are medium-rare. Transfer to a wooden carving platter and loosely cover. (If you prefer medium, cook for another 2 minutes on the second side.) Let rest for 5 to 10 minutes.

3 To make the sauce: Remove all but 2 tablespoons of the drippings from the pan and sauté the shallots over medium-high heat for 1 minute, or until softened, stirring up the brown bits on the bottom of the pan. Add the stock, honey, port, and cherries and increase the heat to high. Reduce the mixture to a light glaze, about 3 minutes. Whisk in the butter to thicken and add sheen to the sauce. Season with salt and pepper.

4 Slice the duck breasts thinly on the diagonal and arrange on serving plates. Spoon over the sauce and serve immediately.

4 boned duck breast halves, with the skin left on (¾ to 1 pound each)

2 tablespoons unsalted butter

sauce

3 medium shallots, minced

¾ cup veal or duck stock

1½ tablespoons orange honey

3 tablespoons tawny port

¾ cup fresh pitted Bing cherries (use frozen if fresh are not available)

1½ tablespoons unsalted butter

Salt and freshly ground black pepper

party prep

This should be prepared through step 1 up to 1 day ahead and refrigerated.

meat entrées

pulled pork

The first time I made this Southern dish, I was surprised at how easy it was to put together. I mean how tough is it to roast pork for 5 hours and then pull it apart with a fork? It's a lot of fun to do this with a friend. Southerners may be appalled at my roasting it rather than barbecuing it, but once you taste it, I think you will agree it is out of this world. The meat steams in the foil while the spice rub gently marinates and tenderizes it.

   This is one of those dishes that is perfect for a large group: in addition to being easy to make, it's really inexpensive, you can make it a few days in advance, and it's a true crowd-pleaser. I like to rub the pork with the spicy mix and let it sit overnight before roasting. I prefer making the sauce but if you are pressed for time, use your favorite barbecue sauce instead. Serve soft white rolls, like Hawaiian sweet bread buns, with the pork. Accompany it with Cabbage & Apple Slaw with Agave-Citrus Dressing (page 83).

serves 16

1 To make the rub: In a small bowl, combine the chili powder, paprika, dry onion, dry mustard, celery seed, salt, pepper, and brown sugar and stir with a fork until completely blended.

2 Cut two pieces of heavy-duty aluminum foil long enough to wrap the pork, and put them on a baking sheet. Place the pork butt in the middle of the foil. Sprinkle the top and sides with half of the rub and gently massage it in. Turn over the meat and massage in the remaining rub. Pull up the foil and carefully wrap it around the meat so that there are no holes or openings in the foil. Put the pork in the refrigerator for at least 4 hours or overnight.

3 Preheat the oven to 300°F. Transfer the pork package to a large Dutch oven and cover the pot. Bake for 5 hours without taking off the lid. After 5 hours, remove the lid. Open the foil and use a spatula to push the meat off as you pull with the other hand to lift out the foil. Return the meat to the oven and roast 1 hour more, or until the top has a crispy crust.

[recipe continues]

rub

2 tablespoons chili powder

1 tablespoon paprika

1 tablespoon minced dry onion or onion powder

1 teaspoon dry mustard

1 teaspoon celery seed

1 tablespoon salt

1 teaspoon freshly ground black pepper

¼ cup packed dark brown sugar

One 7-pound bone-in pork butt

cider vinegar barbecue sauce

2¼ cups apple cider vinegar

2¼ cups ketchup

1½ cups dark brown sugar

¾ cup molasses

1½ tablespoons Worcestershire sauce

¼ cup Dijon mustard

¾ teaspoon cayenne pepper

1½ cups barbecue sauce (your favorite)

1 teaspoon salt

Tabasco sauce (optional)

16 Hawaiian bread buns or any soft bun

4 To make the barbecue sauce: Combine the vinegar, ketchup, brown sugar, molasses, Worcestershire sauce, mustard, cayenne, barbecue sauce, and salt in a large saucepan and whisk to combine. Place the pan over medium-high heat and bring to a boil. Reduce the heat to medium and simmer for about 10 minutes, or until slightly thickened. Season to taste. To make it spicier, add some Tabasco sauce.

5 Remove the pork from the oven (leave the oven on). Place on a large baking sheet and let rest for about 15 minutes. Degrease the Dutch oven and reserve. Using two forks, pull the meat apart. Return to the Dutch oven and pour 3 cups of the sauce over the pork. Mix together and cook for about 10 minutes over medium-low heat to meld the flavors.

6 Warm the buns in the oven for 8 minutes. For each serving, place a bun on a plate and, using an ice-cream scoop, scoop the pork onto the bottom half. Spoon on some additional sauce and cover with the top of the bun.

party prep

The pork may be prepared through step 5 up to 3 days ahead, and stored, covered, in a container in the refrigerator. Reheat the pork gently. You may need to add some water to moisten the pork. Leftovers may be frozen in lock-top plastic bags. Push out all of the air before you seal the bags. Defrost and reheat the pork gently.

THE CLEVER COOK COULD:

- Add a favorite barbecue sauce if the meat becomes dry.

- Use the meat in burritos, tacos, or enchiladas.

- Make hash with the meat.

- Top a pizza with the meat and add some shredded Jack cheese.

seriously simple parties

candied bacon

Some chefs call this candied pig, which sounds pretty funny. It is so good that it's difficult to say how many this really serves. I have allowed two pieces per person. But candied bacon goes fast, so double the recipe for a crowd. Applewood-smoked bacon is tasty as is, but when glazed with brown sugar it takes on another layer of sweet, smoky deliciousness. A large platter of creamy scrambled eggs would be a pleasing accompaniment.

serves 6

12 applewood-smoked bacon strips (½ to ¾ pound)

½ cup light brown sugar

1 Preheat the oven to 400°F.

2 Place a silicone pad or a sheet of aluminum foil with the dull side facing up on a baking sheet. Place the bacon on the baking sheet.

3 Carefully sprinkle about 2 teaspoons of the brown sugar evenly over each slice of bacon, making sure the sugar is evenly distributed.

4 Bake for about 8 minutes. To make sure the strips are candied on both sides, with tongs, slide the unsugared side through the sugar syrup in the pan. (You can also use a silicone brush and brush the strips with the syrup.) Turn over the bacon and bake until the top is nicely browned, almost a golden caramel color, about 7 minutes more.

5 Meanwhile, set a wire rack over some foil. With tongs, place the bacon pieces on the rack and let cool. They should be very crisp. Let cool, about 5 minutes. Arrange on a plate and serve.

party prep
This can be made 4 hours ahead, transferred to a plate, and kept at room temperature. Reheat in the microwave for 30 seconds to 1 minute.

meat entrées

pomegranate-marinated grilled lamb chops

The marinade of pomegranate juice with fresh mint gives a spicy, herbal flavor to the lamb, which is more often paired with pomegranate molasses. This is lovely to serve at a small dinner party. The lamb chops look very sophisticated when they are served with their ends crisscrossed. For an elegant dinner, accompany the lamb with Potato and Wild Mushroom Gratin with White Truffle Cheese (page 165).

serves 4 to 6

1 To make the marinade: In a food processor, combine pomegranate juice, balsamic vinegar, mustard, garlic, chopped mint, agave syrup, and vegetable oil. Season with salt and pepper and process until completely blended and smooth. Taste and adjust the seasonings. Set aside.

2 Put the lamb chops in a large lock-top plastic bag and pour in the marinade. Turn the lamb in the bag to coat it evenly. Press out the air, seal the bag, and refrigerate for at least 30 minutes and up to 8 hours, turning once or twice.

3 Preheat an outdoor grill to medium-high, or preheat an oiled grill pan over medium-high heat. Remove the lamb chops from the marinade and grill for 5 to 7 minutes per side for medium-rare, depending on the thickness of the meat.

4 Place the lamb chops on serving plates, crisscrossing the ends for a pretty presentation. Garnish with the mint leaves and pomegranate seeds. Serve immediately.

party prep

The lamb chops may be prepared up to 8 hours in advance through step 2, covered, and refrigerated.

marinade

½ cup pomegranate juice

2 tablespoons balsamic vinegar

2 tablespoons whole-grain mustard

2 garlic cloves, minced

3 tablespoons finely chopped fresh mint, plus whole leaves for garnish

2 teaspoons agave syrup

¼ cup vegetable oil

Salt and freshly ground black pepper

8 to 12 thick rib lamb chops, up to ¾ inch thick

Pomegranate seeds for garnish

veal stew niçoise

This is a great winter party dish. Create a cozy mood with a crackling fire in your fireplace. You could serve this on a bed of soft, creamy polenta or egg noodles with a few simple Roasted Carrots (page 161) strewn on top. This is what I like to call bowl food—dishes that are all in one bowl and can be eaten on your lap or at the table.

serves 6

1 Preheat the oven to 325°F.

2 Dry the veal on paper towels. In a lock-top plastic bag, season the flour with salt and pepper. Put the veal in the bag, seal it, and shake until the meat is evenly coated.

3 Heat 3 tablespoons of the olive oil in a heavy, deep, flameproof casserole over medium-high heat. Brown the meat on all sides, in batches so as not crowd the pan, turning with tongs, 4 to 5 minutes. Remove the meat to a bowl. (Add more oil as needed to make sure that the pan and meat do not burn.)

4 Add 2 tablespoons of the olive oil to the pan and sauté the onions until lightly browned and softened, about 5 minutes. Add three-fifths of the garlic and sauté for 1 minute more. Add the wine and deglaze the pan, scraping up the browned bits on the bottom. Add the tomatoes and thyme, season with salt and pepper, and bring to a simmer. Return the meat to the pan and mix to combine.

5 Bake the veal for 1½ hours, or until the meat is tender when pierced with a fork.

6 Meanwhile, heat the remaining 1 tablespoon of olive oil and the butter in a large skillet and sauté the mushrooms for 4 to 5 minutes, or until cooked through. Add the remaining garlic and cook for 1 minute more. Season with salt and pepper. Remove from the heat.

7 When the veal is done, remove from the oven and add the mushrooms, olives, and ¼ cup of the parsley. On the stove top, reduce the liquid over high heat for about 5 minutes, or until slightly thickened. Taste for seasoning.

8 Serve the veal in the casserole or place in a serving bowl and garnish with the remaining ¼ cup parsley and the thyme branches.

3 pounds veal stew meat, cut into 2-inch pieces

2 tablespoons all-purpose flour

Salt and freshly ground black pepper

6 tablespoons olive oil, or more if needed

2 onions, finely chopped

5 garlic cloves, minced

2 cups dry red wine, such as Cabernet Sauvignon or Zinfandel

1½ cups canned crushed tomatoes

1 teaspoon fresh thyme leaves, or ½ teaspoon dried, plus thyme branches for garnish

1 tablespoon unsalted butter

1 pound cremini mushrooms, quartered

1 cup pitted Niçoise or Kalamata olives, well drained

½ cup finely chopped fresh parsley

party prep

This may be prepared up to 2 days ahead through step 6, covered, and refrigerated. Reheat gently. Or the dish may be prepared through step 4 and frozen. Defrost, reheat gently, and continue with step 5.

meatball sliders
with tomato sauce

Sliders have become popular in the last few years. I love serving them to a big crowd since they are fun to eat and very economical. These meatballs are incredibly moist and flavorful and fit right into a small hamburger bun, Hawaiian bread bun, or small Parmesan roll. Any meatballs you don't use can be frozen for future bashes. Think of these as the centerpiece of an afternoon of football watching, or offer them as a little bite with a glass of wine.

serves 16 to 24 as a main course or 60 as an appetizer
(makes about sixty 2-inch meatballs)

1 Heat the olive oil in a medium skillet over medium heat. Add the leeks and sauté them for 5 to 7 minutes, stirring frequently, until they're soft and translucent. Sauté the carrots for 1 minute, add the garlic, and sauté for 1 minute more.

2 Cool the cooked vegetables and transfer to a large bowl. Add the eggs, Dijon mustard, chili sauce, parsley, Parmesan, bread crumbs, seasoning salt, and pepper. Blend well, using a large spoon or your hands to mix all the ingredients together. Add the veal, beef, and pork and mix to blend all the ingredients.

3 Preheat the oven to 375°F. Line a few baking sheets with aluminum foil for easy cleanup. With your hands, gently roll the mixture into meatballs about 1½ inches in diameter. Place them on the baking sheets and bake for about 35 minutes, or until cooked through and no longer pink.

[recipe continues]

3 tablespoons olive oil

4 leeks, light green and white parts only, cleaned and finely chopped

2 carrots, peeled and shredded, or 1 cup preshredded carrots

4 garlic cloves, minced

3 large eggs

¼ cup Dijon mustard

1 cup chili sauce

½ cup finely chopped fresh parsley

1 cup freshly grated Parmesan cheese

1 cup fine dried bread crumbs (panko works well)

1 tablespoon Seriously Simple Seasoning Salt (page 217) or store-bought seasoning salt

½ teaspoon freshly ground black pepper

1 pound lean ground veal

1½ pounds lean ground beef (15% fat)

1½ pounds ground pork

Two 26-ounce jars good-quality marinara sauce

¼ cup finely chopped fresh basil

1 teaspoon finely chopped fresh thyme

2 teaspoons balsamic vinegar

60 mini-buns or slider rolls

4 Meanwhile, heat the marinara sauce in a large Dutch oven or a deep skillet large enough to hold all the meatballs. Add the basil, thyme, and vinegar. Bring to a boil, reduce the heat to medium, and cook for 5 minutes. Taste for seasoning. Heat the meatballs in the sauce for about 15 minutes, or until the sauce is coating the meatballs nicely.

5 If the rolls are not precut, cut them horizontally part of the way through. If desired, spread them out on a baking sheet and bake in a 350°F oven until heated through, about 5 minutes. Place a meatball and some of the sauce inside each bun, arrange on a platter, and serve immediately.

party prep

The sliders may be prepared 1 day ahead through step 4, covered, and refrigerated. Reheat on medium heat, basting with the tomato sauce, until the meatballs are hot. The cooked meatballs, without the sauce, can also be frozen.

THE CLEVER COOK COULD:

• Serve the meatballs with 2 pounds of your favorite pasta (it will serve about 12 people).

• Make a meat loaf. Form the meat and vegetable mixture into a large loaf, place it on a baking sheet, and bake it for 1 hour at 400°F. For extra flavor, spoon over some of the sauce while the meat loaf is cooking.

• Make the meatballs spicier by adding some crushed red pepper to the meat and vegetable mixture.

• Freeze some meatballs and add them to your favorite soup.

the perfect burger

We all have our own idea of what makes a perfect burger. For me, it's this combination of juicy medium-rare beef, caramelized onions, and warm, creamy blue cheese. Goat cheese or sharp cheddar are also good. The sauce on the buns brings all of the flavors together. I ask my butcher to grind a combination of half chuck and half brisket, which gives the burgers a deep, rich beefiness.

serves 6

1 To make the sauce: In a small bowl, combine the mayonnaise and steak sauce and mix to blend. Set aside.

2 Gently shape the meat into six thick patties with an indentation in the center of each one. (Do not compress the meat, and handle as little as possible to shape.) Lightly cover with wax paper and refrigerate until ready to grill.

3 Preheat a grill to medium-high. Just before grilling, season the patties with salt and pepper on both sides. Grill the burgers for 3 to 4 minutes on the first side, and then flip over and cook for 4 to 6 minutes on the second side for medium-rare (or cook until desired doneness). Grill the split buns about 4 minutes before the burgers are done. Top the burgers with cheese about 2 minutes before the burgers are done so the cheese can melt.

4 Spread 1 tablespoon of the sauce on both the bottoms and tops of the buns. Place the burgers on the bottom halves of the buns and top each burger with 1 tablespoon onions. Cover with the tops of the buns. Serve immediately.

party prep

The burgers may be made through step 2 up to 6 hours ahead. Cover the sauce and burgers and refrigerate.

sauce

⅓ cup mayonnaise

3 tablespoons good-quality steak sauce

3 pounds freshly ground chuck or beef brisket or half and half (15% fat or more)

Coarse salt and freshly ground black pepper

6 onion or soft hamburger rolls, split

¾ cup crumbled blue cheese or goat cheese, or 6 slices sharp cheddar cheese

½ cup warm Caramelized Onions (page 215)

THE CLEVER COOK COULD:

- Make these into sliders for a cocktail party. Shape the meat into 1½-inch burgers and serve with slider buns.

- Use Thousand Island dressing instead of the sauce.

grilled tri-tip of beef with herb rub

Tri-tip beef is a famous California cut that is often used for grilling. It is very flavorful and just casual enough for a barbecue party. It is equally good hot or cold. Serve it with Roasted Tomato Jam (page 211).

serves 12

(page 211)

1 To make the rub: In a small bowl, combine the seasoning salt, thyme, and chili powder. Mix until well blended.

2 Rub the entire surface of the roasts with the mixture. Place in two lock-top plastic bags and refrigerate for at least 1 hour and up to 24 hours.

3 Preheat the grill to medium-high. Grill the beef for about 3 minutes on each side, or until a crust begins to form. Turn down the grill to medium heat. Cover the grill and cook each side for about 10 minutes more, or until an instant-read thermometer registers 125°F for rare or 130°F for medium-rare. Let the meat rest for 10 minutes before carving.

4 Carve the meat on a diagonal against the grain into 1/2-inch slices. Serve immediately or refrigerate and serve chilled.

party prep

The beef may be made through step 2 up to 1 day ahead and refrigerated. If you want to serve it cold, it may be made completely 1 day ahead, covered, and kept in the refrigerator. Remove from the refrigerator 1 hour before serving.

rub

1/4 cup Seriously Simple Seasoning Salt (page 217) or store-bought seasoning salt

2 tablespoons dried thyme

2 teaspoons chili powder

Two 3-pound tri-tip roasts

beef brisket
with zinfandel & dried fruit

Parties can be as casual as a family dinner. This is my traditional family party dish, since it is always requested. This is also good for any Jewish holiday. Look for the first cut of brisket because it is decidedly leaner than the point cut. Make it 1 or 2 days ahead—you'll have more time to prepare the rest of the menu on the day of the party. Dried fruit adds a subtle fruit flavor to the sauce. The prune juice and balsamic vinegar give it a tangy-sweet kick, while the fire-roasted tomatoes add a hint of smokiness. Serve the brisket with Crispy Potato and Apple Pancakes (page 166) or the Israeli Couscous with Caramelized Leeks, Carrots & Zucchini (page 174).

serves 8

1 Preheat the oven to 325°F. Dry the brisket well and season with salt and pepper on both sides. Heat the olive oil over medium-high heat in a heavy roasting pan large enough to fit the brisket and vegetables. Brown the brisket for about 4 minutes per side, or until nicely browned. (This will assure the sauce has a deep-brown color and a rich flavor.)

2 Toss in the onions, carrots, and garlic. Add the wine, tomatoes, 3 tablespoons balsamic vinegar, $1/2$ cup prune juice, prunes, apricots, and thyme. Mix the ingredients around to combine. Bring to a boil and season with salt and pepper.

3 Remove the pan from the heat. Cover well with aluminum foil and braise in the oven for 3 to $3^{1}/_{2}$ hours, or until fork-tender. Let the brisket cool. (You can refrigerate it so it is chilled and easy to slice.) Remove the meat to a carving platter and slice against the grain $1/4$ inch thick. Place the meat in overlapping slices in a 9-x-13-inch serving dish with at least $1^{1}/_{2}$-inch sides to catch the sauce.

One 5-pound first-cut brisket

Salt and freshly ground black pepper

2 tablespoons olive oil

4 onions, thinly sliced

4 carrots, peeled and sliced

16 garlic cloves, peeled

1 cup dry, medium-bodied Zinfandel

One $14^{1}/_{2}$-ounce can fire-roasted diced tomatoes

3 tablespoons balsamic vinegar, plus 1 teaspoon

$1/2$ cup prune juice, plus 1 tablespoon

$3/4$ cup pitted large prunes

$3/4$ cup medium dried apricots

1 tablespoon finely chopped fresh thyme, or 1 teaspoon dried

2 tablespoons finely chopped fresh parsley for garnish

4 Remove 1 cup of the vegetables (not the dried fruit) from the roasting pan and 1 cup of the liquid and purée in the blender. (To prevent an accident, make sure to hold down the top tightly or take out the inner part of the top so the steam can escape.) Return the purée to the sauce, mix, and add the remaining 1 tablespoon prune juice and remaining 1 teaspoon vinegar. Season with salt and pepper. Stir and taste for seasoning. Pour over the meat. Cover and refrigerate overnight.

5 When ready to finish the dish, preheat the oven to 350°F. Remove any accumulated fat. Reheat until warmed through and bubbling, about 30 minutes. Garnish with the parsley and serve.

party prep

The dish may be prepared up to 3 days ahead, except for the garnish, covered, and refrigerated. This also freezes well. Defrost completely and continue with step 5.

side
dishes

sautéed green beans
in sake brown butter

Sautéing green beans over high heat gives them a rich golden brown color. The sake and brown butter brings out the beans' inherent sweetness. Be sure to buy tender medium-size beans for best results. If you want to make these for a crowd, use a large skillet to sauté the beans.

serves 4 to 6

1 Fill a large saucepan with enough salted water to cover the beans, and bring to a boil. Immerse the beans and cook until tender but slightly resistant to the bite, 5 to 7 minutes. Rinse the beans in cold water to stop the cooking and drain them well.

2 Melt the butter with the sake in a medium skillet over medium-high heat. When the mixture begins to brown, add the beans and toss, using tongs, until they just begin to brown and are heated through, about 3 minutes. Season with salt and pepper and toss to combine.

3 Transfer the beans to a serving dish and serve immediately.

party prep
The beans may be prepared up to 6 hours ahead through step 1, covered, and kept at room temperature.

2 pounds tender green beans, ends removed

2 tablespoons unsalted butter

2 tablespoons sake

Salt and freshly ground black pepper

THE CLEVER COOK COULD:

- Add sautéed mushrooms to the beans when they're done.

- Double or triple the recipe for a crowd.

- Replace the green beans with yellow wax beans or use a combination of the two.

- Add a few tablespoons of Caramelized Onions (page 215) to the beans, tossing to distribute them evenly.

roasted carrots

These simple carrots are roasted to bring out their sweet garden goodness. They are a perfect side dish for most main course dishes. A mound of these rustic, roasted spears adds a splash of color to the dinner or buffet table.

serves 4 to 6

2 pounds medium carrots, peeled and trimmed, with a little green left on

2 tablespoons olive oil

1 teaspoon sugar

1 teaspoon Seriously Simple Seasoning Salt (page 217) or store-bought seasoning salt

2 tablespoons finely chopped fresh parsley

1 Preheat the oven to 425°F.

2 Put the carrots on a large baking sheet. Pour the olive oil over the carrots and sprinkle with the sugar and seasoning salt. Roll the carrots in the oil until evenly coated.

3 Roast the carrots for 20 minutes. Roll them around and roast for another 20 minutes, or until the carrots are cooked through and nicely browned.

4 Remove from the oven and arrange on a serving platter. Garnish with the parsley and serve.

party prep

The carrots may be prepared through step 3 up to 4 hours ahead, loosely covered, and left at room temperature. Reheat at 350°F for about 10 minutes, or until heated through.

roasted brussels sprouts & winter squash

These are a welcome side dish in the cooler months. The firm, slightly brown Brussels sprouts blend nicely with the creamy, bright-orange squash pieces. To gild the lily you could add some pomegranate seeds for a garnish. Serve this with Butterflied Dry-Brined Roast Turkey with Maple Butter (page 138) or Pomegranate-Marinated Grilled Lamb Chops (page 149).

serves 6 to 8

2 pounds medium Brussels sprouts, outer leaves and end removed

2 pounds peeled winter squash, cut into 1½-inch pieces

3 leeks, light green and white parts only, cleaned and thinly sliced

2 teaspoons salt

3 tablespoons olive oil

Freshly ground black pepper

1 Preheat the oven to 400°F. Combine the Brussels sprouts, squash, leeks, salt, and olive oil in a shallow roasting pan (a 12-x-17-inch jelly-roll pan works well) and toss to coat. Season with pepper.

2 Roast the vegetables for 20 minutes. Move them around so they will cook evenly, and roast for another 15 to 20 minutes, or until the vegetables are cooked through and lightly browned. Taste for seasoning.

3 Transfer the vegetables to a serving bowl and serve immediately.

party prep

The dish can be prepared through step 1 and left in the pan, covered lightly with foil, for up to 4 hours before roasting.

THE CLEVER COOK COULD:

- Add ½ pound of freshly cooked and crumbled crispy bacon bits to the roasted vegetables.

- Toss the vegetables with some dried cranberries and Basic Vinaigrette (page 204) and serve as a chilled vegetable salad.

roasted herbed fingerling potatoes

If you can't find fingerling potatoes, just cut larger ones into 1½-inch pieces. These potatoes cook nicely with the skins on, which gives them a rustic, colorful presentation. Serve these with any simple grilled or roasted dish, or with eggs.

serves 6 to 8

1 Preheat the oven to 425°F. Combine the potatoes, olive oil, seasoning salt, pepper, thyme, and rosemary in a shallow roasting pan (a 12-x-17-inch jelly-roll pan works well). Roll the potatoes around with a large spoon or shake the pan from side to side until all the potatoes are well coated with oil and herbs.

2 Roast the potatoes for 20 minutes. Shake the potatoes so they are browning evenly and roast for another 15 minutes, or until the potatoes are brown and crusty. Taste for seasoning.

3 Spoon the potatoes into a serving bowl and garnish with the parsley and thyme and rosemary leaves. Serve immediately.

party prep

The potatoes may be made 2 hours ahead and kept at room temperature. Reheat for about 10 minutes at 350°F, or until hot.

3 pounds red, yellow, and purple fingerling potatoes (about 1½ inches across)

3 tablespoons olive oil

1 teaspoon salt or Seriously Simple Seasoning Salt (page 217) or store-bought seasoning salt

¼ teaspoon freshly ground black pepper

2 teaspoons coarsely chopped fresh thyme, plus extra leaves for garnish

2 teaspoons coarsely chopped fresh rosemary, plus extra leaves for garnish

2 tablespoons chopped fresh parsley for garnish

THE CLEVER COOK COULD:

• Add 12 small shallots to the mixture and roast with the potatoes.

• Make a potato salad with these potatoes. Let the potatoes cool, toss with Basic Vinaigrette (page 204), and serve at room temperature.

potato & wild mushroom gratin
with white truffle cheese

Serve this dish with grilled steaks or roast chicken. You could also make this your go-to vegetarian main course and serve it with Roasted Carrots (page 161) and steamed spinach.

serves 6 to 8

1 Heat the olive oil in a large sauté pan over medium heat and sauté the leeks for 10 to 12 minutes, or until softened and lightly caramelized. Add the mushrooms and sauté, tossing occasionally, for about 5 minutes, or until nicely softened and no liquid remains. Add the garlic and sauté for 1 minute more. Season with salt and pepper. Set aside.

2 Peel the potatoes. Slice ⅛ inch thick—the food processor works well for this, especially with the fine slicing disc. You can also use a mandoline. Put the potatoes in a clean dish towel and wring out as much liquid as you can.

3 In a large, deep sauté pan, season the cream with salt and pepper and then add the potatoes, separating the pieces as you drop them in. Bring to a boil over high heat. Reduce the heat to medium-low and simmer, covered, for 10 minutes, stirring occasionally with a wooden spoon. Remove the lid and continue simmering until most of the cream has been absorbed. (The potatoes should be partially cooked, but still crisp. Watch carefully because the bottom of the pan may burn.) Taste for seasoning.

4 Preheat the oven to 350°F. Oil a 9-x-13-inch baking dish. With a large spoon, transfer half the potato mixture to the dish and spread out in an even layer. Layer the mushrooms on top of the potatoes. Sprinkle evenly with half of the cheese. Cover with the remaining potatoes, and sprinkle the remaining cheese evenly on top.

5 Bake the gratin for 40 to 45 minutes, or until the potatoes are cooked and the top is brown and crusty. (You can check the potatoes by inserting the tip of a sharp knife into them; if they give easily, they are done. If the top browns too quickly, cover loosely with foil.) Let rest at least 10 minutes before cutting into squares and serving.

¼ cup olive oil

3 leeks, light green and white parts only, cleaned and finely chopped

1½ pounds mixed fresh wild mushrooms, such shiitake, chanterelle, black trumpet, morels, porcini, and cremini, in any combination, cleaned and coarsely chopped

2 garlic cloves, minced

Salt and freshly ground black pepper

3 pounds Yukon gold potatoes

2 cups whipping cream

1 cup shredded white truffle cheese

party prep

The dish may be made through step 4 up to 4 hours ahead, covered, and left at room temperature.

THE CLEVER COOK COULD:

- Use half Parmesan and half Gruyère cheese instead of the white truffle cheese.

crispy potato & apple pancakes

These crispy pancakes are a variation on potato latkes, which are traditionally the star dish at a Chanukah party, along with sour cream and applesauce. But latkes are delicious year-round as well. This version combines the russet or baking potato with cubed apple. The starch and moisture in the potato helps the pancakes keep their shape and fry crisply, while the apple adds a faintly sweet flavor. Try serving these with Maple-Cinnamon Applesauce (page 214).

This no-fail method calls for using a food processor instead of grating the potatoes and onion by hand. I purée the eggs and onion in the food processor until fluffy, and then pulse in the potato and apple chunks until they resemble finely grated potatoes. I usually test one in hot oil before I start cooking a batch to make sure that they are seasoned just right.

serves 4 to 6 (makes 12 to 14 pancakes)

1 Purée the onion and eggs together in a food processor until they are smooth and fluffy. Add the potatoes and apple and pulse until the mixture is finely chopped but still retains some texture. Add the flour and baking powder, season with salt and pepper, and quickly process to combine. Do not overprocess. Pour the batter into a medium bowl.

2 Heat ¾ inch of canola oil in a large nonstick skillet over medium-high heat. Pour a tablespoon of batter into the skillet to test the oil. If it is hot enough, the pancake will begin to sizzle and brown. Spoon a few more tablespoons of the batter to the skillet, making sure that there's a little room between the pancakes. Flatten them with the back of a spoon and use the edge of a spatula to round out the sides, if necessary. Fry the pancakes until they are golden brown on one side, and then turn them and brown the other side.

1 medium onion, quartered

2 large eggs

2 medium baking potatoes, peeled and cut into 2-inch cubes

1 Gala apple, peeled and cut into 2-inch cubes

3 tablespoons all-purpose flour

½ teaspoon baking powder

Salt and freshly ground black pepper

Canola oil for frying

1 cup Maple-Cinnamon Applesauce (page 214)

THE CLEVER COOK COULD:

- Make dollar-size pancakes and serve them as an appetizer.

- Serve these with scrambled eggs for brunch.

3 Transfer the pancakes to a baking sheet lined with two layers of paper towels to blot the excess oil. Place the pancakes on a platter and serve with the applesauce.

party prep

To freeze the potato pancakes, cool the pancakes completely and lay them on doubled sheets of aluminum foil. Enclose the pancakes tightly in the foil and then place on a flat surface in the freezer. When ready to serve, preheat the oven to 425°F and place the foil packets on a baking sheet. Remove the top sheet of foil so that the pancakes will bake easily. Bake the frozen pancakes for 5 to 7 minutes, or until they are warm and crispy.

POTATO PANCAKES POINTERS

- Wear old clothes when frying, since you will smell like fried oil when you are finished.

- Use nonstick skillets for easy turning.

- Double or triple the recipe if you are having a crowd. I like to use a small ice-cream scoop to drop the pancakes into the hot oil. You can also use a ladle or large soup spoon.

- Have a flat wire skimmer nearby to collect any particles that remain in the oil. If the oil becomes too dirty, discard and begin again.

- Don't crowd the pan, or the oil temperature will drop and the pancakes will be oily.

- Have a wide spatula for turning them.

sweet potato
purée with coconut milk

Here's a taste combination that is bound to surprise and please your guests. I first tasted a version of this at Spago in Maui and loved it so much that when I got home, I made up my own recipe. This is an interesting mix of tropical flavor and the old-fashioned taste of sweet potato. You can use one variety, but I like to combine the white and the orange types. Make sure to get unsweetened coconut milk so the dish isn't too sweet. Serve it plain or add the gingersnap and coconut topping. This goes beautifully with roast pork, chicken, or turkey.

serves 8 to 12

3 pounds sweet potatoes, half orange and half white, unpeeled

1¼ cups unsweetened coconut milk

2 tablespoons dark brown sugar

Salt and freshly ground white pepper

½ cup unsweetened coconut (optional)

½ cup crushed gingersnaps (optional)

2 tablespoons unsalted butter, chopped (optional)

1 Preheat the oven to 425°F. Put the sweet potatoes on a baking sheet. Bake for 1 hour, or until very soft. Let sit until cool enough to handle. Remove the skin and put the potatoes through a potato ricer or food mill and into a large bowl.

2 Add the coconut milk and brown sugar to the bowl. Season with salt and pepper and mix to combine. Taste for seasoning. You may need to adjust the sugar because potatoes vary in sweetness.

3 Put the puréed potato mixture into a greased 9-inch round or square ovenproof baking dish.

4 Preheat the oven to 350°F. If desired, combine coconut, gingersnaps, and butter in a small bowl and sprinkle over the sweet potato purée.

5 Bake the sweet potato purée for 20 to 25 minutes, or until the top is golden brown and the potatoes are heated through. If the topping starts to get too dark, cover loosely with aluminum foil.

party prep
This may be prepared through step 3 up to 2 days ahead, covered, and refrigerated. Remove from the refrigerator 1 hour before baking.

sweet corn
pudding

I am a sucker for anything that is made with corn. This luscious corn pudding is like a taste of summer. You can serve it right from the oven or at room temperature. It goes well with most chicken, fish, and meat entrées and can be a part of a vegetarian main course as well.

serves 6

1 Preheat the oven to 350°F.

2 Combine 2 cups of the corn kernels, the eggs, half-and-half, basil, cornmeal, flour, baking powder, salt, and pepper in a blender. Blend the mixture until very smooth.

3 Butter a 6-cup (8-inch-square) shallow baking dish. Pour the pudding mixture into the dish and then sprinkle in the remaining 2 cups corn kernels and stir to blend.

4 Put the dish in a larger pan. Put the pan in the oven and then pour enough hot water into the larger pan to come about halfway up the sides of the baking dish.

5 Bake the pudding for 50 to 55 minutes, or until the tip of a knife inserted in the center comes out clean and the top is golden brown. Serve immediately or cool to room temperature and serve.

party prep

The pudding can be made up to 4 hours ahead, covered, and kept at room temperature. If serving hot, reheat in a 350°F oven for 10 to 15 minutes.

4 cups fresh corn kernels (about 4 large or 8 medium ears of corn)

4 large eggs

2 cups half-and-half or whole milk

2 tablespoons finely chopped fresh basil

¼ cup cornmeal

¼ cup all-purpose flour

¼ teaspoon baking powder

1¾ teaspoons salt

½ teaspoon freshly ground black pepper

THE CLEVER COOK COULD:

- For a spicier version, add a finely chopped jalapeño or serrano chile after the mixture has been blended, so there will be tiny pieces of jalapeño in the pudding.

grilled sweet peppers, eggplant & corn

This colorful vegetable mélange makes great use of summer and early autumn produce, bursting with flavors. A large platter of these on the buffet table or served family-style can become the centerpiece. Serve this with any grilled meat, fish, or poultry.

serves 12

1 Preheat the grill to medium-high. Grill the bell peppers until charred on all sides, 7 to 10 minutes. Transfer to a paper bag and fold over the top to close tightly. Let steam for 10 minutes. Peel and seed the peppers, and cut into 1/2-inch-thick strips. (I use a pizza cutter to do this.) Reserve.

2 Brush the eggplant slices with olive oil and grill on each side for 3 to 4 minutes, or until the eggplant slices have grill marks and feel soft. Remove to a plate.

3 Brush the corn with olive oil and sprinkle with salt and pepper. Grill until charred in spots, turning occasionally, about 10 minutes. Transfer to a large bowl and cover to keep warm.

4 Heat the 1/4 cup olive oil in a large skillet over medium-high heat. Add the bell pepper strips. Sauté until heated through, stirring often, 3 to 5 minutes. Stir in the 1/2 cup basil. Season with salt and pepper.

5 Arrange the eggplant slices in the bottom of a large shallow platter, leaving room in the center. Spoon the peppers into the center and arrange the corn on the edge of the platter. Garnish with the remaining 2 tablespoons basil and serve.

party prep

The dish may be prepared through step 2 up to 1 day ahead, covered, and refrigerated. Warm in a 350°F oven until heated through, about 10 minutes.

---

4 red bell peppers

4 yellow bell peppers

4 Japanese eggplants, sliced 1/2 inch thick

olive oil for brushing the eggplant and corn, plus 1/4 cup

9 large ears of corn, each broken in half

Salt and freshly ground black pepper

1/2 cup finely chopped fresh basil, plus 2 tablespoons

THE CLEVER COOK COULD:

- Cut leftover roasted corn off the cob, toss with defrosted frozen edamame, and mix with Edamame Pesto (page 208).

- Use any remaining vegetables as a base for a chopped salad. Chop the vegetables, and add chopped arugula and romaine. Dress with Basic Vinaigrette (page 204). Add cooked chicken or shrimp for a more substantial main course salad.

- Purée leftover vegetables with vegetable broth and fresh herbs and chill. Serve as a cold soup.

- Use any remaining peppers and eggplant for sandwiches.

black beans
with chorizo & chipotle cream

Black beans are a versatile, inexpensive party side or main dish. Here, Mexican spices like cilantro and cumin, and jalapeño chile impart a spicy Latin flavor to the simple, simmered beans. A sauté of onions and chorizo sausage adds another layer of flavor. (See the Clever Cook for vegetarian options.) I always serve this with Mexican Seafood & Scallion Sauté with Mango-Avocado Salsa (page 118) for a casual Mexican dinner menu.

serves 6 to 8

1 To make the chipotle cream: Combine the sour cream, Tabasco, and lime juice in a small bowl and blend with a whisk. Season with salt. Cover and refrigerate.

2 Soak the beans in plenty of water for at least 4 hours or overnight. Drain.

3 Combine the beans, bay leaf, oregano, and onion halves in a medium pot. Add enough cold water to cover generously. Bring to a boil on high heat. Reduce the heat to medium and simmer, uncovered, checking a few beans frequently, until very tender but not falling apart, 1 to 1½ hours, depending on the age of the beans. Drain the beans, reserving 1½ cups of the cooking liquid. Remove the onion halves and bay leaf.

4 In a large nonstick skillet with high sides, heat the vegetable oil over medium heat. Brown the chorizo for about 4 minutes, or until cooked through. Remove to a small bowl and reserve. Add the chopped onions to the skillet and sauté, stirring occasionally, for 12 to 15 minutes, or until softened and golden brown. (You may need to add another tablespoon of oil). Add the garlic, jalapeño, cumin, and chopped cilantro and cook for 1 minute more.

chipotle cream

½ cup sour cream

1 to 2 teaspoons Tabasco chipotle sauce

2 teaspoons fresh lime juice

Salt

2 cups dried black beans

1 bay leaf

1¼ teaspoons dried oregano

3 medium onions; 1 halved, 2 finely chopped

2 tablespoons vegetable oil

¼ pound spicy fresh Mexican chorizo sausage, casing removed

2 garlic cloves, minced

½ small jalapeño chile, cored, seeded, and minced (see note)

½ teaspoon ground cumin

2 tablespoons finely chopped fresh cilantro, plus extra leaves for garnish

Salt

5 Add 1 cup of the reserved bean cooking liquid, the chorizo, and drained beans to the skillet and stir to mix thoroughly. If you need more liquid, add the remaining ½ cup of the bean cooking liquid. The beans should have a bit of juice, but should not be soupy. Cook the beans to heat through, about 2 minutes.

6 Remove 1 cup of beans, mash with a fork, and then return them to the pan. Season with salt. Transfer to a serving bowl and garnish with the chipotle cream and cilantro leaves. Serve immediately.

party prep

The entire recipe may be prepared up to 2 days ahead. Cover the chipotle cream and the beans and refrigerate. Bring to room temperature and reheat gently before serving. Taste for seasoning.

note

When working with chiles, always wear rubber gloves. Wash the cutting surface and knife immediately afterward.

THE CLEVER COOK COULD:

- For a vegetarian main course, omit the chorizo sausage and add some smoky Tabasco chipotle sauce to the beans before step 6. Serve the beans alongside Grilled Sweet Peppers, Eggplant & Corn (page 171) or Sweet Corn Pudding (page 169) with plenty of warm tortillas.

- Use this as a filling for burritos or enchiladas.

israeli couscous
with caramelized leeks, carrots & zucchini

When you need a side dish that works with strong-flavored entrées, this is it. Israeli couscous, a baked semolina wheat pasta, is larger than regular couscous and tastes great sautéed and lightly browned. The vegetables add some welcome texture and color.

serves 6

1 Heat the olive oil in a medium saucepan over medium heat. Add the leek and sauté for 5 to 7 minutes, or until lightly browned. Add the carrot and zucchini and continue to sauté for 2 minutes, or until slightly softened. Increase the heat to medium-high and add the couscous. Sauté the couscous until lightly browned, for about 3 minutes, stirring constantly. Season with seasoning salt.

2 Add the hot water to the couscous, stir with a fork, and bring to a boil. Cover and reduce the heat to medium-low. Let the couscous simmer for about 10 minutes, or until all the liquid has been absorbed and the couscous is tender.

3 With a large fork, blend in the parsley and Parmesan (if using). Season with pepper and serve immediately.

party prep
The dish may be prepared up to 2 hours ahead and kept at room temperature. Reheat carefully in the top part of a double boiler over medium heat for 10 minutes.

2 tablespoons olive oil

1 leek, light green and white parts only, cleaned and finely chopped

1 carrot, peeled and finely diced

1 zucchini, finely diced

2½ cups Israeli couscous

Seriously Simple Seasoning Salt (page 217) or store-bought seasoning salt

2 cups hot water or chicken or vegetable broth

2 tablespoons finely chopped fresh parsley

2 tablespoons freshly grated Parmesan cheese (optional)

Freshly ground black pepper

THE CLEVER COOK COULD:

- Add toasted pine nuts or almonds just before serving.

- Make this into a salad. Add diced turkey, chicken, or tuna to the mixture and moisten with Basic Vinaigrette (page 204).

- Using the same technique, cook long-grain rice. Increase the liquid to 4 cups and cook for about 20 minutes, or until the rice is done. This will serve 8.

desserts & sweets

limoncello zabaglione
with fresh berries

This is a really good, quick dessert. As long as I have these few ingredients in my pantry, I know I can prepare the zabaglione for a last-minute get-together. Limoncello is an Italian lemon liqueur that pairs beautifully with the egg custard. This light and frothy sauce is wonderful over fresh berries or cut-up summer fruit like peaches, nectarines, or plums. Serve some amaretti cookies alongside.

serves 6 (makes about 1¼ cups of custard)

zabaglione

6 egg yolks

3 tablespoons sugar

⅓ cup limoncello

1 tablespoon crème fraîche or sour cream

6 cups of your favorite berries, such as blueberries, raspberries, blackberries, or thinly sliced strawberries, or sliced stone fruit

Fresh mint sprigs for garnish

1   To make the zabaglione: In the top of a medium double boiler, combine the egg yolks, sugar, and limoncello and whisk until well blended. Place the double boiler insert over gently boiling water, over medium heat, and whisk the mixture vigorously until it becomes foamy and begins to thicken, 4 to 6 minutes. Remove from the heat and let cool for 10 minutes. Add the crème fraîche and whisk until incorporated. The consistency should be thick and custardlike and should coat a spoon.

2   Put the berries in a mixing bowl and toss. Spoon the fruit into individual small bowls (wine goblets look pretty). Pour on the zabaglione, garnish with mint sprigs, and serve immediately.

party prep
You can serve the zabaglione chilled. It may be prepared up to 6 hours ahead. Cover and refrigerate and make sure to whisk it right before serving.

pomegranate & orange granita

I love this refreshing iced dessert. It's pretty— the granita looks like little shards of jeweled ice—and it makes a light ending for a lunch or dinner. The granita needs to be made ahead, so plan accordingly. It's best to serve this at sit-down parties, since the granita melts quickly. The dessert looks especially lovely in glass dessert bowls.

serves 6 to 8

3 cups sweetened pomegranate juice

3 cups fresh orange or tangerine juice

¾ cup agave syrup

Fresh mint leaves for garnish

1 Combine the pomegranate juice, orange juice, and agave syrup in a large bowl and whisk together to blend. Transfer to a shallow 8-cup plastic or glass container with a tight-fitting lid. Cover securely so it will not leak.

2 Put the mixture in the freezer and freeze for 4 hours. Remove from the freezer and remove the top. Drag a fork across the mixture, breaking it up so it resembles granules of ice. Freeze again until serving.

3 Remove the granita from the freezer a few minutes before serving. Drag a fork across the mixture once again, breaking it up so it resembles granules of ice.

4 Scoop the granita into small dessert dishes, garnish with mint leaves, and serve immediately.

party prep
This may be made through step 2 up to 2 days ahead.

caramel coconut ice-cream terrine

Made in a loaf pan, this fancy ice-cream dessert looks pretty with a couple of overlapping slices arranged on a plate and the sauce drizzled on top. Sweet, slightly tropical, and refreshing all at the same time, this is a make-ahead dessert.

serves 6 to 8

1 Line a loaf pan (approximately 8½ x 5 x 3 inches) with a piece of plastic wrap long enough to cover the loaf completely.

2 To make the sauce: Combine the sugar and 2 tablespoons of water in a heavy, deep medium saucepan over medium-low heat. Holding the handle of the saucepan, swirl the mixture around until the sugar dissolves. Increase the heat to high. Boil until the mixture turns dark amber, about 4 minutes, occasionally swirling the mixture and brushing down the sides of the pan with a wet pastry brush. Remove from the heat. Immediately add the cream and whisk to incorporate (the mixture will bubble vigorously). Then add the cream of coconut. Whisk over low heat until blended with the caramel and the sauce is smooth and slightly thickened, about 4 minutes. Let cool (it will thicken more as it cools).

3 Preheat the oven to 350°F. Spread out the flaked coconut evenly on a small baking sheet. Bake until golden brown, stirring every 3 to 4 minutes, about 12 minutes total (watch the coconut carefully to make sure it does not burn). Set aside to cool.

4 In a large bowl, use a large spoon to combine the ice cream with ¾ cup of the toasted coconut until they are blended together. Spoon the filling into the prepared loaf pan, smoothing it down until it is in an even layer. Spoon ¼ cup of the caramel on top of the ice cream and swirl with a wooden skewer. Wrap the plastic over the top of the ice cream. Freeze for at least 8 hours or overnight.

5 When ready to serve, reheat the caramel sauce in a small saucepan over low heat. Remove the loaf pan from the freezer 5 minutes before serving. Take the ice cream out of the loaf pan and remove the plastic. Cut the ice cream into enough slices so that each person will have two, and overlap the slices on dessert plates. Spoon some of the warm caramel sauce over each slice. Sprinkle with the remaining coconut, and serve immediately.

coconut caramel sauce

½ cup sugar

½ cup whipping cream

½ cup sweetened cream of coconut

1½ cups sweetened flaked coconut, loosely packed

3 pints vanilla ice cream, softened at room temperature for 30 minutes

party prep

The caramel sauce and terrine may be prepared up to 3 days ahead of serving. Freeze the terrine, and cool, cover, and refrigerate the caramel sauce.

chocolate-peppermint pots de crème

This rich French-style chocolate pudding is silky and luxurious. I like to put each serving in an espresso cup on a small plate with a doily and a demitasse spoon—perfect for a sit-down party. This is an elegant dessert that easily can be doubled. The peppermint extract adds a bit of a holiday flavor. If you're not a fan of peppermint, use a teaspoon of orange liqueur instead and garnish with some orange zest.

serves 6

1 In a large saucepan, heat the half-and-half over medium-high heat until it comes to a simmer. Remove the pan from the heat and add the chocolate. Whisk until the chocolate is totally melted and blended into the half-and-half.

2 In the bowl of an electric mixer, beat the egg yolks until frothy. Slowly add the sugar and peppermint extract and beat until thick and a light lemon color, 3 to 4 minutes.

3 Whisk the chocolate mixture into the egg yolk mixture and continue whisking until well blended. Return the combined mixture to the pan and cook over low heat for about 3 minutes more, or until the mixture coats a spoon. Remove from the heat.

4 Strain the mixture into a pitcher (I use a 6-cup Pyrex measuring cup), and then carefully pour into six 3- to 5-ounce espresso cups, custard cups, or ramekins. Refrigerate until set and cold, at least 4 hours.

5 Garnish each pot de crème with a dollop of crème fraîche and some crushed peppermint candy. Serve immediately.

2 cups half-and-half

1 pound bittersweet chocolate, cut into small pieces, or bittersweet chocolate chips

6 egg yolks

$\frac{1}{3}$ cup sugar

1 teaspoon peppermint extract

Crème fraîche for garnish

Crushed peppermint candies or candy cane or whole fresh mint leaves for garnish

party prep

The puddings can be made up to 2 days ahead, covered, and refrigerated. Garnish just before serving.

chocolate caramel matzo brittle

This sweet is not just for the Passover holidays; it's delicious all year long. Surprise your guests with a plate of matzo brittle after dinner in the fall or winter. It will be a conversation starter for sure. That said, it does make a great gift for the host of a Passover seder.

I like to make this up ahead of time and keep it refrigerated until serving. Look for disposable baking sheets for easy cleanup. You can double the recipe, but you will have to make the caramel in two separate batches. Serve this on its own or with a bowl of ripe spring strawberries.

serves 8 to 12 (makes 4 sheets)

1 Preheat the oven to 400°F. Line two baking sheets with foil or parchment paper. Or, to avoid a messy cleanup, place a disposable baking sheet on top of each of the baking sheets. Put 2 matzos on each baking sheet.

2 In a medium saucepan over medium heat, melt the butter. Add the brown sugar and stir well. (If the heat is too high the mixture will burn.) Simmer, whisking constantly, for about 3 minutes, or until the mixture becomes thick and caramel-like. Remove from the heat.

3 Working quickly so that the caramel doesn't harden, divide the caramel mixture among the sheets of matzo. Use a metal spatula to spread the mixture evenly over the entire surface of each matzo.

4 Place the matzos in the oven and bake for about 5 minutes, or until the topping is bubbly and brown. Watch carefully so it doesn't burn.

5 Remove from the oven and immediately sprinkle each matzo evenly with the chocolate chips. Return the matzos to the oven for about 2 minutes more, or until the chocolate is just melted. Remove from the oven and spread the chocolate evenly over each matzo with a spatula. Sprinkle evenly with the almonds.

6 Refrigerate the matzos for at least 1 hour, or until the chocolate has hardened. Break into pieces or cut into strips and arrange on a platter to serve.

4 sheets matzo

6 tablespoons unsalted butter or margarine

½ cup dark brown sugar

¾ cup bittersweet chocolate chips

⅓ cup toasted almond slices

party prep

The matzo brittle may be prepared up to 1 week ahead, stored in an airtight container, and refrigerated. It can also be frozen.

desserts & sweets

doughnut muffins

I first tasted these heavenly muffins at the Downtown Bakery and Creamery in Healdsburg, California. With a texture that is closer to a doughnut than a muffin, these sweet nuggets are really easy to make. They remind me of cinnamon-sugar doughnuts without the deep-frying fat or mess. The biggest decision you'll have to make is whether you want mini-muffins or large ones. Sometimes when I can't decide, I make some of each. I bake 6 large doughnut muffins and 24 mini-muffins. These little treats make a great breakfast or brunch addition. If I am having young children over, I try and time the muffins to come out of the oven when they arrive, so they can help roll them in cinnamon sugar—a fun activity for kids *and* adults.

makes 48 mini-muffins or 12 regular muffins

1   Preheat the oven to 375°F. Butter and flour four mini-muffin pans or one regular muffin pan.

2   In a large bowl, whisk together the flour, baking powder, salt, nutmeg, and baking soda. In a small bowl, whisk together the milk, buttermilk, and eggs until well blended.

3   In the bowl of an electric mixer, beat the room-temperature butter and ¾ cup plus 2 tablespoons of the sugar together on medium speed until light yellow and the sugar granules can't be seen, 4 to 5 minutes. Decrease the mixing speed to low and add the dry ingredients and milk mixture in thirds, alternating between the two and beating after each addition to incorporate it into the batter. Stop beating once the batter is completely mixed. Do not overmix or the muffins will be tough.

[recipe continues]

3 cups all-purpose flour

2½ teaspoons baking powder

¾ teaspoon salt

½ teaspoon freshly grated nutmeg

¼ teaspoon baking soda

¾ cup whole milk, at room temperature

2 tablespoons buttermilk, at room temperature

2 large eggs

10 tablespoons unsalted butter, at room temperature, plus ½ cup (1 stick), melted

1¾ cups plus 2 tablespoons sugar

1 tablespoon ground cinnamon

4 Using a small ice-cream scoop for mini-muffins or a regular ice-cream scoop for large muffins, fill the prepared muffin cups, just up to the top, with the batter. Bake for 13 minutes for mini-muffins or 17 to 18 minutes for regular muffins, or until a skewer inserted in the middle of a muffin comes out clean. Do not worry if the tops of the muffins have not browned. Remove the muffins from the oven and cool for 10 minutes on a wire rack lined with foil or wax paper.

5 In a small bowl, combine the remaining 1 cup sugar and the cinnamon. Put the melted butter in another small bowl. Set up an assembly line with the muffins, melted butter, and sugar mixture. Dip a muffin in the butter or brush the muffin with butter, coating it lightly all over. Try to get the sides of the muffin, so it will have more topping. Then coat all over liberally with the cinnamon-sugar. Shake off the excess and transfer to a serving platter. Repeat with the remaining muffins. Serve immediately.

party prep

These are best eaten warm. You can make them 1 day ahead and keep them in an airtight container.

THE CLEVER COOK COULD:

- Fill a pastry bag fitted with a small tip with a mixture of peanut butter and jelly for kids or just jelly. Use the tip to poke a small hole in the bottom of each muffin and fill it. This works best with large muffins.

- Use the remaining buttermilk to make Buttermilk Garden Herb Dressing (page 205).

seriously simple parties

puff pastry almond fruit tarts

These tarts are easy to make and impressive to look at. Your guests will think you are a professional baker.

The puff pastry is cut into 6 rectangles, but if you like, you can cut it into 12 small squares for little puffs. If you are not an almond lover, omit the marzipan and almonds and just include the fruit. You can easily double this recipe for a larger party of 12. For a buffet, present these on a large platter with a dessert spatula for serving.

serves 6

1 Preheat the oven to 400°F. Line a baking sheet with parchment paper. Defrost the pastry sheet for about 40 minutes, or until soft enough to open.

2 Unfold the pastry sheet onto a lightly floured surface. With a pizza cutter, cut into six equal rectangles, working quickly to ensure the dough stays chilled and does not become too sticky to handle. With a spatula, transfer the pastry to the baking sheet.

3 With a knife, lightly score a border about 1/8 inch from the edges of each rectangle, being careful to not cut through the dough. Make three slits in the middle of each rectangle without cutting through the bottom.

4 Sprinkle some of the marzipan evenly over each pastry shell, leaving the scored border uncovered. Arrange a thinly sliced half of a peach or nectarine or a whole fig over the marzipan. (You can also mix the fruits together.) With a clean finger, moisten the edges of each pastry evenly with the egg wash.

5 Bake the tarts for 20 to 22 minutes, or until the pastry is brown and puffed.

6 Remove from the oven and place the tarts on a wire rack to cool.

7 While the pastry is cooling, heat the apricot jam in a small microwave-safe bowl in the microwave for about 30 seconds, or until thinned out. Brush over the fruit and then sprinkle with the almonds. Arrange the tarts on a platter and serve.

One 10-x-9-x-1/8-inch frozen puff pastry dough sheet

1/2 cup crumbled marzipan (slice the marzipan and then crumble with your fingers)

3 medium peeled peaches or nectarines, or 6 fresh figs, thinly sliced

1 large egg beaten with 2 tablespoons milk or water for an egg wash

1/2 cup apricot jam

1 tablespoon thinly sliced almonds

party prep

This may be made 4 hours ahead and kept at room temperature. You can also reheat this in a 325°F oven for 5 minutes.

THE CLEVER COOK COULD:

Try these combinations of fruits, nuts, and jams for different seasons

- Fresh apricot pieces glazed with apricot jam and garnished with chopped pistachios

- Peeled and sliced apples or pears glazed with apricot jam

summer stone fruit cobbler

Fruit cobblers are easy to make and always receive rave reviews. A cobbler by definition is a fruit mixture with biscuitlike dough cooked on top of it. Partially cooking the filling prior to adding the cobbler dough helps the dough cook evenly.

This version takes advantage of summer's sweet stone fruit crop. I like the combination of slightly tangy plums and sweet, juicy peaches or nectarines. You can adapt this recipe to your favorite seasonal fruits of the moment. Follow the quantities suggested for the fruit for best results, and make sure to add enough sugar to sweeten the fruit you are using.

serves 6 to 8

1 Preheat the oven to 400°F. Butter and flour a 9-x-13-inch baking dish.

2 To make the filling: Combine the fruit, sugar, lemon zest, and flour in a large bowl and mix well to combine. Spoon into the prepared dish. The fruit should be about $\frac{1}{2}$ inch from the top of the dish so there is room for the cobbler dough.

3 Put the dish on a baking sheet. Bake for 20 minutes, or until hot and bubbly.

4 To make the dough: In a medium bowl, combine the ground almonds, flour, sugar, baking powder, baking soda, and salt. Cut in the butter with your fingers, a pastry cutter, or two knives until it's the size of small peas. In a small bowl, combine the buttermilk, vanilla, almond extract, and egg and whisk to combine. Pour the liquids into the center of the dough mixture and mix with a wooden spoon to combine. The dough will be sticky.

filling

6 large or 10 medium yellow or white peaches or nectarines, cut into 1½-inch pieces (about 10 cups)

4 purple or yellow plums, or a combination, cut into 1½-inch pieces (about 3 cups)

¼ cup sugar

1 teaspoon finely chopped lemon zest

1 tablespoon all-purpose flour

cobbler dough

½ cup ground almonds (almond meal)

1½ cups all-purpose flour

¼ cup plus 2 tablespoons sugar

1½ teaspoons baking powder

1 teaspoon baking soda

½ teaspoon salt

6 tablespoons chilled unsalted butter, cut into ¼-inch pieces

¾ cup buttermilk

1 teaspoon vanilla extract

½ teaspoon almond extract

1 large egg

1 tablespoon sugar

2 tablespoons sliced almonds

French vanilla ice cream for serving (optional)

5 When the fruit has cooked for 20 minutes, remove it from the oven and place on a heat-proof counter. Use an ice-cream scooper to drop the dough onto the hot fruit. You can spread out the dough and make it as even as you like. The more uneven the dough, the more cobbled it will look. Sprinkle the 1 tablespoon of sugar and the sliced almonds over the dough.

6 Return the cobbler to the oven for about 20 minutes more, or until it is golden brown and the dough is cooked through. Let cool for 30 minutes on a rack and serve with ice cream, if desired. The cobbler is best served warm.

party prep

The cobbler can be prepared up to 8 hours ahead and kept at room temperature. Serve at room temperature or reheat in a 350°F oven for 10 to 15 minutes.

THE CLEVER COOK COULD:

- Use apples and pears with a touch of pumpkin pie seasoning for a cold-weather version.

rhubarb & strawberry crostata

Surprise your guests with this one-crust, free-form pie filled with tart rhubarb, sweet strawberries, and a touch of fresh ginger. Rhubarb is one of those flavors that can be very polarizing. People seem to either love or hate rhubarb, which has a natural affinity for strawberries. The two flavors meld beautifully. Make sure to peel or scrape the outer skin off so that the rhubarb is easy to eat. I have found that cutting the rhubarb into pieces smaller than the strawberries will result in a perfectly cooked dessert. A scoop of vanilla ice cream would be a tasty finish. If possible, serve this warm.

serves 6

1 To make the crust: Combine the flour, salt, and sugar in a food processor and process for about 5 seconds. Add the butter and a few tablespoons of the water and process until the dough has a crumblike texture, 5 to 10 seconds. Add more water if the dough isn't moist enough to hold together and process briefly again. Pat the dough into a disk for easy rolling. Cover in plastic wrap and refrigerate for 30 minutes.

2 Put the removable bottom of a 10-inch springform or tart pan on a heavy baking sheet with a rim. The baking sheet will catch the tart's juices (you won't need the sides of the springform or tart pan for this free-form tart). On a floured surface, roll out the pastry into a 13-inch round. Roll the pastry loosely around the rolling pin and transfer it to the tart pan bottom, laying the dough flat to cover the bottom, with a 3-inch border of dough overhanging its edge. Refrigerate while making the filling. Preheat the oven to 400°F.

crust

1¼ cups all-purpose flour

¼ teaspoon salt

1 teaspoon sugar

½ cup (1 stick) frozen unsalted butter, cut into ½-inch pieces

4 tablespoons ice water

filling

¼ cup sugar

2 tablespoons all-purpose flour

½ pound rhubarb, peeled and cut into ¼-inch slices

1 pint strawberries, hulled and cut into ½-inch pieces

1 teaspoon grated lemon zest

1 teaspoon minced peeled fresh ginger

3 tablespoons sugar

1 tablespoon all-purpose flour

1 pint French vanilla ice cream (optional)

3 To make the filling: In a medium bowl, combine the sugar, flour, rhubarb, strawberries, lemon zest, and ginger.

4 Remove the crust from the refrigerator and sprinkle 2 tablespoons of the sugar and the 1 tablespoon flour evenly over the center of the crust. Arrange the fruit mixture in the center of the pastry and then fold about 3 inches of the pastry edges up around the fruit, making pleats, so it looks like a free-form tart. Brush the pastry with water and sprinkle the remaining 1 tablespoon sugar evenly over the pastry and fruit.

5 Bake the tart for 40 to 45 minutes, or until the fruit filling is bubbling and the crust is nicely browned. Let cool at least 20 minutes on a wire rack. Transfer the tart, still on the pan bottom, to a serving platter. Slice and serve with ice cream, if desired.

party prep

The tart may be prepared up to 8 hours ahead, loosely covered, and kept at room temperature. To serve, preheat the oven to 325°F and reheat the tart for about 10 minutes, or until heated through.

THE CLEVER COOK COULD:

* Replace the rhubarb and strawberries with apples or pears in the cooler months. Figure about 4 peeled and sliced apples or pears instead of the summer fruit. You can vary the spices, depending on the fruits you choose. Make sure to adjust the amount of sugar, depending on the sweetness of the fruit.

desserts & sweets

strawberry shortcake
with white chocolate whipped cream

Almost everyone loves strawberry shortcake, so it's usually a popular party dessert. My take on this homespun dessert includes a modern garnish of white chocolate whipped cream. These shortcakes aren't rolled out. Instead the batter is scooped and quickly rolled into balls, which are very sticky to the touch; be prepared to get a bit messy. The strawberries are sugared and kept at room temperature so their intense flavor can shine. The white chocolate whipped cream adds a delicious touch to the berries and shortcakes. It is best to serve these warm. You can either present the cakes at the table and get everyone involved by having your guests add the topping, or serve the shortcakes completely finished.

serves 6

1 Preheat the oven to 425°F.

2 To make the dough: In a large bowl, combine the flour, sugar, baking powder, and salt and whisk together to blend the ingredients well. Add the butter and mix into the dry ingredients with your fingers, two knives, or a fork until the butter is the size of peas. In a small bowl, combine the milk, sour cream, egg, lemon zest, and vanilla. Whisk until well blended. Make a well in the center of the flour mixture and add the liquid ingredients. Stir together, gradually mixing the flour into the well, until all the flour is incorporated. The dough will be very moist. Cover the dough and let rest for 15 minutes.

3 Meanwhile, in a medium bowl, combine the strawberries with 2 tablespoons of the sugar. Cover and leave at room temperature.

dough

2 cups all-purpose flour

3 tablespoons sugar

2½ teaspoons baking powder

½ teaspoon salt

6 tablespoons very cold butter, cut into ½-inch pieces

½ cup milk

½ cup sour cream

1 large egg

Zest of 1 lemon

1 teaspoon vanilla extract

3 pints strawberries, hulled and thinly sliced

3 tablespoons sugar

3 ounces good-quality white chocolate

1½ cups whipping cream

1 large egg beaten with 1 tablespoon milk for an egg wash

4   Put the white chocolate in a small microwave-safe bowl. Microwave for about 90 seconds on high power or until melted. Let cool for 1 minute.

5   In a medium bowl, whip the cream with an electric mixer on medium speed until soft peaks form. Add the white chocolate and fold into the cream. Whip the cream until stiff peaks form. Cover and refrigerate.

6   Grease a baking sheet. Flour your hands and, using a small scoop or a large tablespoon, scoop a small ball (about 3 inches in diameter) of dough into your hands. Roll to form a round ball, working quickly. Place on the baking sheet. Repeat with the remaining dough until you have six shortcakes. Lightly flatten them with your hand. Brush each cake with the egg wash and sprinkle evenly with the remaining sugar.

7   Bake the shortcakes for about 20 minutes, or until golden brown. Cool on a rack.

8   Cut each cake in half horizontally. Place the bottoms on a serving plate. Spoon some of the berries over each bottom. Spoon a dollop of the whipped cream over the berries, and then partially cover with the top of the shortcake, so you can still see some cream and strawberries. Serve immediately.

party prep

The whipped cream can be made up to 4 hours ahead, covered, and refrigerated. The strawberries may be made 2 hours ahead, covered, and kept at room temperature. The shortcakes can be made up to 4 hours ahead and reheated in a 325°F oven for 5 to 10 minutes, watching carefully so they do not burn.

THE CLEVER COOK COULD:

* Replace the strawberries with other berries, such as blueberries or raspberries, or with chopped peaches or nectarines.

* Double this recipe for a larger group.

desserts & sweets

blueberry streusel buttermilk coffee cake

Coffee cakes are perfect for brunch or for a casual dessert party (as well as a late night snack or a breakfast nibble). This tender spiced cake, studded with juicy blueberries and topped with a golden, crispy streusel, has a special place in my recipe file. I prefer to bake this in a lightweight nonstick Bundt pan because it cooks more evenly, but you can also bake it in a 9-x-13-inch baking pan. You can use fresh or frozen blueberries. Fresh berries will fall to the bottom of the cake and create a blueberry jam–like layer. Frozen berries will be more evenly distributed in the batter. Whether served in squares stacked on a cake platter or produced right from a Bundt pan, this comforting sweet will be a pleasant addition to any breakfast, brunch, or tea menu.

serves 10 to 12

1 To make the streusel: Combine the brown sugar, cinnamon, flour, and pecans in a medium bowl and stir together. Add the butter. With two knives, your fingers, or a pastry blender, cut the butter into the dry ingredients until the mixture resembles large bread crumbs. Set aside in the refrigerator until ready to use.

2 To make the cake: Preheat the oven to 350°F. Butter and flour a 12-cup nonstick Bundt pan or a 9-x-13-inch baking pan and set aside.

3 Combine 2 cups of the flour, the baking powder, baking soda, and salt in a medium bowl. Set aside.

4 In the bowl of an electric mixer, beat the butter on medium speed until light and fluffy. Gradually add the sugar, continuing to beat until very light. Add the lemon zest and then add the eggs, one at a time, beating well before adding the next one. (Don't overbeat or the cake will be tough.)

streusel

¾ cup light brown sugar

1 teaspoon ground cinnamon

¾ cup all-purpose flour

¾ cup finely chopped pecans

6 tablespoons cold unsalted butter, cut into 1-inch pieces

cake

2¼ cups all-purpose flour

1 teaspoon baking powder

1 teaspoon baking soda

½ teaspoon salt

½ cup (1 stick) unsalted butter, at room temperature

1 cup sugar

Zest of 1 lemon

3 large eggs

1¼ cups buttermilk

2½ cups fresh or frozen blueberries

Powdered sugar for dusting the cake (optional)

5 With the mixer on low speed, alternately mix in the flour mixture and the buttermilk in thirds, beating just until the batter is blended, and set aside.

6 In a medium bowl, combine the remaining ¼ cup flour and the blueberries. Toss until the blueberries are thoroughly coated. Sift out any remaining flour with your fingers. Gently fold the blueberries into the batter.

7 If using a Bundt pan, spoon half of the batter into the pan and sprinkle with a third of the streusel. Cover with the remaining batter and smooth out to make an even layer. Sprinkle the remaining streusel evenly over the top. Pat it down gently. If using a rectangular pan, spoon in all of the batter and then sprinkle evenly with the streusel topping, patting it down gently.

8 Bake until the top of the cake is firm and the streusel is crisp and golden brown (a skewer inserted into the center of the cake should come out clean), 40 to 45 minutes for a 9-x-13-inch pan, and 55 to 60 minutes for a Bundt pan.

9 Cool the cake for 15 minutes in the pan on a wire rack. If using a Bundt pan, invert the cake onto a wire rack, and then reinvert it onto a serving platter so that the streusel side is on top. If using a rectangular pan, cut the cake into squares and present them on a serving platter. Dust the cake with powdered sugar, if you like, before serving.

party prep

The cake can be prepared up to 1 day ahead, covered loosely, and kept at room temperature.

mocha celebration cake

My dear friend Denny Luria shared this recipe with me, and now it has become our family tradition for many celebrations. This cake consists of one large round layer, which makes it easy to frost and serve. It looks beautiful sitting on a large cake platter. I have also served it for summer buffet luncheons and at dessert parties. You will need a 12-inch round cake pan, which you can find at any cookware or restaurant supply store. Look for the chocolate-covered espresso beans at a gourmet food shop. If you have any of this left over, you can freeze it and slice it after it has defrosted.

serves 12 to 16

1 To make the ganache frosting: Combine the sugar and cream in a large saucepan over medium-high heat, stir to combine, and bring to a boil. Reduce the heat to medium-low and simmer for 3 minutes. Remove from the heat. Add the chocolate, coffee, vanilla, and butter and blend together, stirring constantly until the chocolate and butter are completely melted. Let cool and then cover. Refrigerate until the frosting has thickened, at least 1 hour.

2 To make the cake: Preheat the oven to 350°F. Grease and flour a 12-inch round cake pan. Line the edges of a 14-inch round platter with 3-inch-wide strips of wax paper, which you will remove after frosting the cake.

3 Sift the flour, baking powder, baking soda, and salt into a medium bowl. Sift the cocoa into a small bowl so it has no lumps, and then transfer to a heat-proof 2-cup measuring cup. Pour the boiling coffee over the cocoa and stir to dissolve.

[recipe continues]

ganache frosting

¾ cup baker's or ultrafine sugar

¾ cup whipping cream

5 ounces good-quality unsweetened chocolate, cut into pieces

¼ cup strong coffee

1 teaspoon pure vanilla extract

6 tablespoons unsalted butter, cut into small cubes and chilled

cake

2 cups all-purpose flour

1 teaspoon baking powder

1 teaspoon baking soda

¼ teaspoon salt

1 cup plus 3 tablespoons good-quality unsweetened cocoa powder

1 cup boiling coffee

3 large eggs

2 cups baker's or ultrafine sugar

1½ sticks (¾ cup) unsalted butter, at room temperature

1 cup buttermilk

1 teaspoon pure vanilla extract

Chocolate-covered espresso beans for garnish

4 In the bowl of an electric mixer, combine the eggs and sugar and beat on medium speed until the sugar is dissolved, about 2 minutes. Add the butter and beat for another 1 minute, until blended. Add the buttermilk and vanilla and blend again for 1 minute. Add the cocoa mixture and beat until incorporated and no streaks remain, about 1 minute. Add the flour mixture and mix until blended, about 1 minute.

5 Pour the batter into the prepared cake pan and bake for about 40 minutes, or until a cake tester comes out clean.

6 Let the cake cool completely in the pan on a rack and then invert it onto the serving platter.

7 With a metal spatula, frost the top and sides of the cake very thickly with half of the ganache frosting. Let sit for 10 minutes to firm up, and then frost with the remaining ganache. Remove the strips of wax paper and use a damp paper towel to remove any excess frosting from the platter. Let the frosting set. Arrange a pretty design of chocolate espresso beans on the cake, and serve at room temperature.

party prep
The cake may be prepared up to 1 day ahead, loosely covered, and left at room temperature.

brownie toffee cookies

My guests often request these chewy, fudgy cookies. The toffee bits add a bit of extra sweetness and texture to the bittersweet chocolate batter. Easy to make, these chocolate bites are equally delightful at an afternoon tea, casual lunch, or dinner party. Sometimes I serve these after the meal on a pretty platter with coffee and liqueurs. It makes a relaxing end to the evening.

makes about 30 cookies

1 cup all-purpose flour

¼ teaspoon salt

¼ teaspoon baking powder

4 tablespoons unsalted butter

1¼ cups bittersweet chocolate chips

⅔ cup semisweet chocolate chips

3 large eggs

¾ cup sugar

1 teaspoon vanilla extract

½ cup toffee bits

1 Preheat the oven to 350°F. Grease and flour two baking sheets, or line the baking sheets with parchment paper.

2 In a small bowl, sift together the flour, salt, and baking powder and set aside.

3 Melt the butter and bittersweet and semisweet chocolate chips in the top of a double boiler over boiling water. Whisk the butter and chocolate until blended and cool.

4 In a medium bowl, beat the eggs and sugar with an electric mixer on medium-high until lemon colored, about 1 minute. Add the chocolate mixture and the vanilla and beat until combined. Stir the flour mixture into the batter gradually, so there will be no lumps. Stir in the toffee bits.

5 Use a small ice-cream scoop to scoop out 1½-inch mounds of dough, and place them about 3 inches apart on the prepared baking sheets. Dip the ice-cream scoop in hot water before scooping each cookie to prevent sticking.

6 Bake the cookies for 10 to 12 minutes, or until the tops barely spring back and are slightly puffed. Transfer to a rack and cool. Store in an airtight container for up to 3 days until serving.

party prep

The cookie dough can be made through step 4, covered, and refrigerated for up to 1 day before continuing with step 5.

shortbread
with chocolate & candied walnuts

These cookies are really simple to prepare and are always a crowd-pleaser. It's easy to find candied walnuts or pecans, so no need to make them from scratch. Since the cookies are quite rich, small squares are the perfect serving size. Present these on a pretty platter. A bowl of berries would be a nice accompaniment. If you keep some of these in your freezer, you'll have an instant dessert for any impromptu gathering.

makes 16 squares

1 Preheat the oven to 350°F. Line an 8-inch square baking pan with a piece of foil long enough to press up the sides of the pan, with a 1-inch overhang so you can pull the shortbread out in one piece.

2 Melt the butter in a medium saucepan. Remove from the heat and add the brown sugar and vanilla, stirring until smooth. Add the salt and flour, incorporating it gradually and stirring until thoroughly mixed. Spread the mixture into an even layer on the bottom of the prepared pan. Bake for about 20 minutes, or until the shortbread is golden brown.

3 Remove the shortbread from the oven and sprinkle the chocolate chips over the hot shortbread. Return the shortbread to the oven for 1 to 2 minutes, or just until the chocolate has softened. Remove from the oven and spread the chocolate evenly with a metal spatula. Sprinkle the candied walnuts evenly over the chocolate.

4 Place the pan on a wire rack and cool the shortbread slightly for 20 minutes. Then transfer the pan to the refrigerator to cool for about 40 minutes, or until the chocolate has hardened. Lift the shortbread out of the pans and cut into 16 pieces with a serrated knife. Arrange on a platter and serve.

½ cup (1 stick) unsalted butter, cut into cubes

½ cup dark brown sugar

1 teaspoon pure vanilla extract

¼ teaspoon salt

1 cup all-purpose flour

1 cup bittersweet chocolate chips

½ cup candied walnuts, chopped

party prep

The shortbread may be prepared up to 1 month ahead and stored in an airtight container in the freezer. Defrost at room temperature for about 15 minutes before serving. They may also be kept up to 3 days in an airtight container at room temperature or in the refrigerator.

THE CLEVER COOK COULD:

- Double the recipe for a larger party. It is best to use two 8-inch pans rather than one larger one.

- Present the shortbread in cellophane bags tied with ribbon as party favors.

- Use different candied nuts or use toasted nuts instead.

basics

basic vinaigrette

Keep this on hand in your refrigerator. It's great not only as a salad dressing but also as a light sauce for fish or vegetables. You can double or triple this recipe.

makes 1 cup

1 Combine the shallot, garlic, parsley, chives, mustard, lemon juice, and red wine vinegar in a medium bowl and whisk until well blended. Or, combine in a food processor and process until well blended.

2 Add the olive oil into the bowl in a slow, steady stream, whisking constantly (or processing) until blended. Season with salt and pepper.

The vinaigrette may be prepared up to 1 week ahead, covered, and refrigerated. Bring to room temperature and whisk before using.

1 medium shallot, finely chopped

1 garlic clove, minced

1 tablespoon finely chopped fresh parsley

1 tablespoon finely chopped fresh chives

1 teaspoon whole-grain mustard

1 tablespoon fresh lemon juice

3 tablespoons red wine vinegar

¾ cup extra-virgin olive oil

Salt and freshly ground black pepper

THE CLEVER COOK COULD:

- Replace the red wine vinegar with another vinegar, such as red or white balsamic, or pomegranate.

- Add different fresh herbs, such as basil, mint, or cilantro.

- Add 1 or 2 tablespoons of plain nonfat yogurt for a creamier dressing.

- Add diced cucumber, avocado, or tomato and use the vinaigrette as a sauce for fish or vegetables.

buttermilk garden herb dressing

A bit like ranch dressing, but with a punch of fresh herbs and rice wine vinegar, this is my go-to dip for raw vegetables. Drizzle a bit of Balsamic Syrup (page 206) into the dressing for a pretty presentation. I also like to use this as a dressing for a salad of simple romaine lettuce, shredded carrots, and yellow and red cherry tomatoes.

makes 2 cups

Combine the yogurt, mayonnaise, buttermilk, garlic, mustard, vinegar, chives, dill, and parsley in a medium bowl and whisk until completely blended. Season with salt and pepper.

The dressing may be prepared up to 5 days in advance, covered, and refrigerated.

½ cup plain Greek nonfat yogurt

½ cup mayonnaise

1 cup buttermilk

1 medium garlic clove, minced

1 teaspoon Dijon mustard

1 teaspoon rice wine vinegar

1 tablespoon finely chopped fresh chives

1 tablespoon finely chopped fresh dill weed

I tablespoon finely chopped fresh parsley or basil

Salt and freshly ground white pepper

balsamic syrup

I keep this by my stove in a small glass bottle that pours easily. Here is the basic version to get you started. Try experimenting and coming up with your own. You'll find that the syrup really perks up soups and sauces. Drizzle it over grilled beef or chicken.

makes about ¾ cup

Pour the vinegar into a small heavy saucepan over high heat. Reduce the vinegar for 12 to 14 minutes, or until it becomes syrupy. Bubbles will begin to form. (Be careful not to reduce it too much, or it will become burnt and stringy.) Cool the syrup and use a funnel to pour it into a container with a spout. Keep at room temperature. Use as a flavor enhancer for sauces.

The syrup may be made up to 2 months in advance and kept, covered, at room temperature.

2 cups balsamic vinegar

THE CLEVER COOK COULD:

- Add orange or lemon zest to the bottle and then pour in the hot syrup and let it steep. Use on berries, in a vinaigrette, and on grilled chicken and fish.

- Add a few cloves of garlic to the bottle and then pour in the hot syrup and let it steep. Use with fish or chicken, in meat sauces and vinaigrettes, and on cooked vegetables.

seriously simple parties

port & balsamic syrup

This is particularly good over any fruit.

makes about ⅓ cup

Combine the vinegar and port in a small heavy saucepan over high heat. Reduce for 6 to 7 minutes, or until it becomes syrupy. Bubbles will begin to form. (Be careful not to reduce it too much, or it will become burnt and stringy.) Cool the syrup and use a funnel to pour into a container with a spout. Keep refrigerated until using.

The syrup may be made up to 1 month ahead, covered, and refrigerated.

½ cup balsamic vinegar

½ cup tawny port

THE CLEVER COOK COULD:

- Use as a sauce or drizzle for fruit desserts.

edamame pesto

This condiment adds a couple of unusual ingredients to a basic pesto recipe. Marcona almonds and edamame (green soybeans) are incorporated into a creamy, mild, but flavorful paste, accented with the fresh taste of lemon zest. If you love basil, add ¼ cup of fresh basil leaves and process it with the other ingredients.

makes about 1½ cups pesto

1 In a food processor, mince the garlic and almonds. Add the edamame, parsley, cheese, and lemon zest. Pulse until the ingredients are blended but the mixture is still coarse.

2 Add the olive oil in a slow, steady stream and blend until emulsified but some texture remains. Season with salt and pepper.

The pesto may be prepared up to 1 week ahead, covered in an airtight container, and refrigerated.

1 garlic clove, peeled

¼ cup Marcona almonds

1 cup frozen shelled edamame, defrosted

2 tablespoons chopped fresh parsley

¼ cup freshly grated Parmesan cheese

2 teaspoons grated lemon zest

½ cup extra-virgin olive oil

Salt and freshly ground black pepper

THE CLEVER COOK COULD:

- Add the pesto to ricotta cheese for a great dip for crackers or vegetables.

- Add it to a simple vinaigrette.

- Toss with warm pasta. Add some edamame to the pasta as well.

- Use as a spread on sandwiches.

- Add it as a topping to soups.

sun-dried tomato pesto

When you have the time, make this up and keep it in the fridge. It is a wonderful flavor enhancer for soups and sauces. It is also great in pasta and as a topping for puff pastry bites.

makes about ½ cup

2 garlic cloves, peeled

½ cup oil-packed sun-dried tomatoes, drained, plus 1 tablespoon of the oil or 1 tablespoon olive oil

2 tablespoons finely chopped fresh basil

Salt and freshly ground black pepper

2 tablespoons freshly grated Parmesan cheese

In a food processor, with the motor running, combine the garlic with the tomatoes and basil. Season with salt and pepper and process until a thick paste is formed. (If it is too thick, you may need to add a bit more oil.) Transfer the pesto to a container, cover, and refrigerate. Add the cheese just before serving.

The pesto may be prepared up to 1 week ahead, covered, and stored in the refrigerator.

grilled tomato aioli

This sauce is great for roasted or grilled meats or fish or as a dip for vegetables. It's also good as a salad dressing or sandwich spread.

makes about 1 cup

1 Heat a grill pan over medium-high heat. Coat the pan with cooking spray and place the tomato slices in the pan. Grill the tomato on the first side until it has dark grill marks, 3 to 4 minutes. Turn the tomato over and grill for another 2 minutes, or until grill marks appear but the tomato still holds together. Remove the skin and let cool.

2 In a food processor with the motor running, finely mince the garlic cloves. Add the tomato slices and process until well blended. Add the mayonnaise and process until smooth. Add the basil, lemon juice, and cayenne. Season with salt and pepper and process to combine. Taste for seasoning before serving.

The aioli may be prepared up to 5 days ahead, covered in an airtight container, and refrigerated.

1 medium ripe tomato, sliced 1 inch thick

4 medium garlic cloves, peeled

¾ cup mayonnaise

2 tablespoons finely chopped fresh basil, or 1 teaspoon dried

1 teaspoon fresh lemon juice

Salt and freshly ground white pepper

Pinch of cayenne pepper or ancho or chipotle chile powder, or a dash of Tabasco chipotle sauce

roasted tomato jam

If you've never roasted a tomato, you should try it. The juices slowly evaporate, leaving the tomatoes sweet and slightly caramelized. I usually make this in the summer and early fall months, when tomatoes are as they should be—juicy, vine-ripened, and full of flavor.

    While this rustic condiment requires a long cooking time, it needs little hands-on attention. Having tomato jam close at hand will give you easy ways to spruce up simple grilled dishes for party fare. Serve the jam warm on simply flavored chicken breasts or grilled seafood or beef. It's also good on warm pasta. Or try it in scrambled eggs.

makes 1½ cups

6 pounds tomatoes (about 6 large), peeled and coarsely chopped

4 garlic cloves, finely chopped

2 tablespoons olive oil

1 teaspoon finely chopped fresh thyme

Salt and freshly ground black pepper

1 Preheat the oven to 425°F. In a large nonreactive baking pan, combine the tomatoes, garlic, olive oil, and thyme and mix until well blended. Roast for 2 to 2½ hours, stirring every 30 minutes. The liquid will slowly evaporate, and the mixture will begin to thicken and lightly caramelize.

2 Remove the tomatoes from the oven and let cool. Season with the salt and pepper.

The tomato jam may be prepared up to 1 month ahead, covered in an airtight container, and refrigerated.

sautéed cherry tomato relish

This colorful cooked relish makes a pretty side dish to accompany eggs, fish, or chicken.

makes about 1½ cups

1 Cut any tomatoes that are large in half so they are all about the same size.

2 In a medium skillet, heat the olive oil over medium heat. Add the shallot and sauté for 4 to 5 minutes, or until translucent. Add the garlic and sauté for 1 minute more. Add the tomatoes to the pan and cook for 8 to 10 minutes, or until the skins are just beginning to fall off and the shallot is almost softened. Season the mixture with salt and pepper. Remove from the heat and stir in the parsley.

The relish may be prepared through step 1 up to 4 hours ahead, covered, and kept at room temperature.

1 pint yellow and red cherry tomatoes, stems removed

2 tablespoons olive oil

1 medium shallot, finely chopped

1 garlic clove, minced

Salt and freshly ground black pepper

2 tablespoons finely chopped fresh parsley

romesco sauce

You'll find this sweet pepper and almond sauce a welcome Seriously Simple condiment. Use it as a dip, a marinade, or a sauce for fish or chicken.

makes about 1½ cups

In a blender, combine the roasted peppers, almonds, bread, garlic, and pimentón and blend until puréed. Slowly add the olive oil and blend until the mixture is emulsified. Add the salt and pepper and a little water if the sauce is too thick. Taste for seasoning before serving.

The sauce may be prepared up to 1 week ahead, covered in an airtight container, and refrigerated.

½ cup jarred roasted red bell peppers, peeled and seeded

3 tablespoons Marcona almonds

1 slice white bread, crusts removed and bread cut into small pieces

2 garlic cloves, peeled

1 teaspoon pimentón dulce (sweet smoked Spanish paprika) or regular paprika

1 cup extra-virgin olive oil

1 teaspoon salt

½ teaspoon freshly ground black pepper

maple-cinnamon applesauce

I like to make this all-American condiment with maple syrup instead of sugar for a slightly different flavor. Remember that the sweetness of the applesauce will depend, in part, on the sweetness of the apples. So take a bite before cooking. Combining the soft-textured Gala with the crisp pippin or Granny Smith apple results in an applesauce with a more varied texture.

The apples are covered during the first stage of cooking, which essentially steams them, and then uncovered so that the liquid can reduce and intensify in flavor. Serve this as a side dish for brisket or potato pancakes.

makes about 4 cups

1 Combine the apples, maple syrup, cinnamon, and lemon juice in a heavy nonreactive saucepan over medium heat. Cover and simmer for about 12 minutes, or until the apples are slightly softened.

2 Uncover and continue cooking, stirring occasionally to break up the large pieces of apple, for 7 to 10 minutes, or until the apples are soft but still have some texture. (Taste and add more syrup, ground cinnamon, or lemon juice as needed.) Remove from the heat, let cool, and chill before serving.

The applesauce can be prepared up to 1 week ahead, covered, and refrigerated.

3 Gala apples, peeled, cored, and cut into 2-inch chunks

3 pippin or Granny Smith apples, peeled, cored, and cut into 2-inch chunks

¼ cup plus 2 tablespoons maple syrup

1 tablespoon ground cinnamon

1 tablespoon fresh lemon juice

THE CLEVER COOK COULD:

* Use Asian pears instead of the Gala apples.

* Purée with an immersion blender for a fine applesauce instead of a chunky one.

* Use honey or agave syrup instead of the maple syrup.

caramelized onions

Caramelized onions make a tasty addition to many dishes. I try to keep some in my refrigerator when I am giving a party so I can perk up vegetables, add them to eggs, or use them for an appetizer.

makes about 1½ cups

1   Heat the olive oil in large nonreactive sauté pan or Dutch oven over medium-high heat. Add the onions and sauté, stirring frequently, for 12 to 15 minutes, or until well softened.

2   Add the wine, balsamic vinegar, and sugar; reduce the heat to low; and simmer until almost all of the liquid has evaporated and the onions are very tender and caramelized, about another 30 minutes. Season with salt and pepper. Cool the onions and serve at room temperature.

The onions may be prepared up to 1 month ahead, covered in an airtight container, and refrigerated.

¼ cup olive oil

4 large yellow, red, or Maui onions, or a combination, thinly sliced

¾ cup red wine

¼ cup balsamic vinegar

1 tablespoon sugar

Salt and freshly ground white pepper

THE CLEVER COOK COULD:

• Use the onions as a filling for omelets and frittatas, or add them to dips.

• Add these to cooked vegetables such as green beans, spinach, broccoli, or cauliflower.

• Use as a topping on pizza or toasted rustic bread.

parmesan bagel crisps

These bagel crisps are a simple and affordable addition to a brunch or lunch menu. For brunch, serve them with Thyme & Gruyère Egg Puffs (page 108), for example. And for lunch, they make a crispy accompaniment for soups or salads. The cheese and pepper give these crisps the perfect amount of bite!

makes 16 crisps

1 Preheat the oven to 400°F.

2 Using a serrated knife, carefully slice each bagel horizontally into four thin slices. Arrange the bagels on two baking sheets lined with foil. Lightly coat the bagels with olive oil cooking spray to help them crisp up in the oven.

3 Bake the bagels for 12 minutes, or until slightly crispy and golden brown. Remove from the oven. Cover the bagel crisps evenly with the cheese and season with pepper. Bake for an additional 7 minutes, or until the cheese has melted. Watch carefully to ensure the cheese does not burn.

The crisps can be made up to 3 days ahead and stored in an airtight container at room temperature.

4 bagels, plain or onion

1½ cups freshly grated Parmesan cheese

Freshly cracked black pepper

THE CLEVER COOK COULD:

- Use triangles of pita instead of bagels.
- Add fresh herbs to add some color and dress up the chips.

seriously simple parties

seriously simple seasoning salt

This magic seasoning agent will elevate the flavor of just about anything you are cooking. If you make up a batch of this, it will last you for months. I have made a version of this for years, but the process has become easier than ever with the help of a food processor. Purchase peeled whole garlic cloves when you want to make this up quickly. If the mixture is quite wet, add a bit more salt. It does not need to be refrigerated.

makes about 3½ cups

1 In a food processor with the motor running, finely mince the garlic.

2 Combine all the remaining ingredients in a large measuring cup and add to the garlic. Pulse on and off until the mixture is completely blended, using a rubber spatula now and then to move the ingredients around. Transfer to one or two small containers with shakers on the top, and store the rest in a large airtight container.

This will last at least 3 months stored in airtight containers at room temperature.

1 large head garlic, peeled, or 30 medium peeled garlic cloves, ends cut off

2 cups kosher salt

1 tablespoon onion powder

2 tablespoons paprika

3 tablespoons good-quality chili powder

2 tablespoons ground white pepper

2 tablespoons celery seed

1 tablespoon ground ginger

1 tablespoon poultry seasoning

1 tablespoon dry mustard

1 tablespoon dried dill weed

index

table of equivalents

The exact equivalents in the following tables have been rounded for convenience.

LIQUID/DRY MEASUREMENTS

U.S.	METRIC
¼ teaspoon	1.25 milliliters
½ teaspoon	2.5 milliliters
1 teaspoon	5 milliliters
1 tablespoon (3 teaspoons)	15 milliliters
1 fluid ounce (2 tablespoons)	30 milliliters
¼ cup	60 milliliters
⅓ cup	80 milliliters
½ cup	120 milliliters
1 cup	240 milliliters
1 pint (2 cups)	480 milliliters
1 quart (4 cups, 32 ounces)	960 milliliters
1 gallon (4 quarts)	3.84 liters
1 ounce (by weight)	28 grams
1 pound	448 grams
2.2 pounds	1 kilogram

LENGTHS

U.S.	METRIC
⅛ inch	3 millimeters
¼ inch	6 millimeters
½ inch	12 millimeters
1 inch	2.5 centimeters

OVEN TEMPERATURE

FAHRENHEIT	CELSIUS	GAS
250	120	½
275	140	1
300	150	2
325	160	3
350	180	4
375	190	5
400	200	6